ENDORSEM

A Portrai

C000133531

How does one person live with such a succession of tragedies? And yet Cheryl Christopher found a way to redeem pain by speaking to others who go through trials. Bless you and this book as it goes out. I know the book will touch hurting people.

— Philip Yancey,
best-selling author of
Where Is God When It Hurts?
and *What's So Amazing About Grace?*

I have never read a more powerful book—period. This was written by God through the fingers of love. A love deeper than the well of human emotion. This book is a treasure to us all. It is literally God's gift through Cheryl Christopher to you.

— David Cook,
best-selling author of
Seven Days in Utopia: Golf's Sacred Journey
and producer of movie of that name

Cheryl Christopher crafted more than a treatise through the worst storms of grief; more than a textbook; more than moving stories. She did all of that and so much more. I read a few pages and before I knew it, I felt tears on my cheeks.

Everyone who has deeply suffered should read this book or have it read to them. And share it with a friend.

— Jim Hiskey,
Lifetime Member PGA of America.
Author of *Winning is a Choice*
and *What is the Good News Jesus Proclaimed*,
Co-founder the C.S. Lewis Institute and Senior Fellow

Cheryl Christopher's *A Portrait of Grief* is written for those whose story takes them to the unthinkable and sometimes unbearable pain and darkness of grief. Her own experiences of loss and grief will help the grieving souls who find their way to her gracious and comforting words.

Her own experiences of what followed her loss, pain, anger, and questions of faith surrounding personal tragedy are woven into a tapestry of enduring faith and hope. Cheryl's story reminds us that God is still good and can still be found, trusted, and enjoyed, even in despair. Her wisdom and insights will undoubtedly help thousands of people who find themselves in their own portrait of grief.

— John R. Wayland, Jr.,
Senior Pastor of Northwest Bible Church, Spring, Texas,
Area and Regional Director of Young Life,
Author of *A Daily Passage Through the Psalms*
and *A Daily Passage Through Mark*.

Our lives are full of people who come and go, but every so often someone comes into our life who will jar the even tenor of our ways, and our lives will never be the same. Cheryl and Gary Christopher are people who have come into our lives and changed us for good.

Their story is real, and their suffering is overwhelming. They have lived life lessons that have ultimately made them stronger but have also helped others gain strength through their unique grief. They have exhibited the Rock upon which they stand. That Rock is their everlasting faith in Jesus.

The story you are about to read is meant for you so that the life and trials of the author will enable you to fly again in answer to her prayer and yours as well. God loves to answer those kinds of prayers. You will be blessed in this reading.

— Randy Wolff
Executive Director of Wind River Ranch,
Regional Director of Links Players International Golf Ministry,
author of *Fireside Stories for the Soul, Our Daily Light,* and
Moments of a Lifetime.

When you see the smiling face of Cheryl Christopher in the back of this book, you would never imagine the journey she and her family have been through.

Somehow the Christophers have survived. God has reached down, and they have reached up, leading them to a place today where Cheryl can share their story of loss and pain and hurt — in a beautiful way that will touch your heart.

— Pete Hiskey,
friend and pastor to the world of golfers

A PORTRAIT OF

GRIEF

*Hope and Healing
after the Loss of a Child*

BY CHERYL CHRISTOPHER

A Portrait of Grief: Hope and Healing after the Loss of a Child

Trilogy Christian Publishers
A Wholly Owned Subsidiary of Trinity Broadcasting Network
2442 Michelle Drive, Tustin, CA 92780

Cover design: Mike Rhodes, Rhodes Design.
Cover Photograph: "Oaks of Righteousness" by Gary Christopher, 2017.

For information about special discounts for bulk purchases, please contact Trilogy Christian Publishing.

Manufactured in the United States of America
10 9 8 7 6 5 4 3 2 1
Library of Congress Cataloging-in-Publication Data is available.

ISBN: 978-1-63769-924-9
E-ISBN: 978-1-63769-925-6

DEDICATION

To our children and grandchildren, who are with us:
Monty and Holly, Molly and Davis,
Alana, Lila, Carson, Tyce, John Davis, Cross, and Raines.
You brighten our days and sweeten our lives.

In loving memory of our children, who await us:
Austin, Wes, and Brock.
We are closer to reunion with each passing day.

ACKNOWLEDGMENTS

A book is never a solitary endeavor. Although my name appears on the cover, a cast of supporting family, friends, and professionals helped me make the message so much better.

First and predominately, to my husband, Gary, who has lived through most of these stories with me. God keeps blessing me through you with each passing year. Your optimism has provided an environment for faith, hope, and love to grow again. Your loving imprint on my life has been undeniable. Thank you for reading the material over and over and assuring me of the value of the message. Thank you for crying with me and for holding me when the memories got to be too much. Let's keep dancing!

And then to my children, Monty and Molly. You were both a part of the journey from the start. I know your own losses run deep, but oh, how you have ministered to me. Thank you both for your suggestions and advice. Thank you for your willingness to relive some of your worst days and for sharing your hardest memories. I love you both dearly.

I owe a debt to some of my first readers and treasured friends, who offered criticism and encouragement along the way. Thank you, David Cook, Pete Hiskey, Philip Yancey, Loraine and Jim Hiskey, Beth and Bill Rogers, Jeff Hopper, John Wayland, Carol and Randy Wolff, Jim Barker, Linda Brock, Joy Crenshaw, and Mary Milligan.

Thank you to my new friends and prayer warriors who have taken me and my project on as their own. Thank you: Lesley, Diana, Cyd, Gail, Janie, Keith, Linda, Patty, and my newest prayer supporter, Kay-Kay. You are all surely a gift that only God could give.

My editor and writing coach, Keith Wall, deserves a special word of thanks. Keith quickly moved from an advising professional into the realm of a treasured friend. Thank you for all your expertise, wise guidance, and personal support. Your corrections, suggestions, and affirmations written not in red ink but in blue (my favorite color) kept me centered on the true north of God's Word and prevented the book from being a thousand pages long. Your patient and gentle encouragement lifted me up when I was weary of words. It has been a privilege and a joy to work with you, Keith. You are simply the best.

Thank you to my friends at Trilogy Publishing for helping me navigate through the very confusing world of publishing.

Lastly, thank you to our friends and loved ones who did all the right things in the worst of times.

TABLE OF CONTENTS

INTRODUCTION

From Heartache to Healing

You come to this book with a broken heart, crushed dreams, and a deeply wounded spirit. You come not looking for quick fixes or magic formulas to overcome sorrow—because you know there are none. You come, I believe, seeking a small measure of comfort and humble guidance offered by someone who has walked the long path of sorrow and can put an arm around you as you attempt steps forward.

Perhaps you have not lost a child; you have lost your dearest friend, your husband, a parent, your job, or your health. You, too, have an empty place in your heart. You, too, are asking the questions that accompany grief. This book is also for you.

It takes courage even to take this step of reading about the journey ahead. And I commend your bravery for picking up a book on grief and healing. I say that because as much as I love books—and I do love books—I found it impossible to read after losing my child.

When I was young, my mother escorted me downtown to the Tyrrell Public Library every two weeks. There, I would carefully select the maximum number of books allowed to get me through until our next visit. I loved the way the books looked, the way they smelled, and the way they felt. Mostly I loved the people and animals that lived within their pages.

My favorite section of the library held the "orange biographies," a fictionalized series on famous Americans. I wanted to read every one of them, and there were hundreds.

From books, I learned not to tell a lie and that some pigs are terrific, radiant, and humble. I learned that women could fly and that slavery was wrong. Books helped me raise my babies, taught me to cook, and encouraged me on the narrow way of faith. Books have blessed me in innumerable ways.

Like many ardent readers, I have always wanted to write a book. Writing has always seemed the ultimate way to enter the lives of others and to make a difference. I imagined myself writing a self-help book about taking care of aging parents or fashion design or maybe even a cookbook. Never did I imagine that my book would focus on the topic of losing a child.

Following the death of our youngest son, friends arrived with armloads of books on grief and mourning. I could not read them. The traumatic stories of others were more than I could absorb. I didn't care if and how others had lost their loved ones. The loss experienced by my husband and me was the only one that mattered.

Reading is difficult in the midst of grief because concentration is impaired, to put it mildly. Grieving is more demanding and more exhausting than we could ever imagine. There is a preoccupation with all we have lost. It is as though our minds have no space for any other thoughts—nor does anything else have meaning. And yet, there exists a desperation to understand what is happening and where it is all leading us.

In an effort to make this book helpful and easily read, I have structured the material in short chapters. These are like a string of beads—separate writings strung together to create a lifeline to grasp and pull you forward.

Also included are musical suggestions for listening at your own time and convenience. I recommend these because I found that the pain of grief cries out for musical accompaniment. Music helps us to feel the sadness, express it, and move through it. Music is healing and therapeutic, bringing peace to anguished hearts. The songs are accessible on YouTube. If it's too much for you right now, listening is not required.

Feel free to jump around on these pages or to read straight through. The story of our losses is told briefly at the beginning of the book in the first three chapters. If you would prefer to go right to my gentle reflections and practical guidance, feel free to skip over the stories and come back to them another time.

This book has taken me more than twenty years to write. It began in countless journal entries and scribbled notes from my darkest days. I am not a psychiatrist nor a psychologist, although I have met with many bereaved parents. And by now, I have read scores of works on bereavement. My credentials are simply that I am a person of faith who asked God "Why?" myriad times, endured perhaps the most painful of all losses a person can experience, and eventually found the strength to stand up and take steps forward.

Most of all, I can offer the hope and belief that you, too, will find the strength and courage to take tiny steps into a brighter future.

"Why has it taken you so long to write this?" you might ask.

Not only does catastrophic loss cripple, but it also creates tremendous chaos. Everything changes. Everything is turned upside down. The death of a child changes perspectives on life, it changes our values, and it changes all of our relationships.

My husband and I changed homes, churches, and I changed vocations several times. We owned and operated a second-generation photography business, which had been in continuous operation for sixty-five years. We sold our business and moved to another community and then to another. We found new friends, retired far too early, and learned new ways to fill our days. It takes a lot of time and energy to process so many life changes.

A part of me went missing for a long time only to be found and then lost again and again. Many external things give form and structure to how we perceive ourselves. In losing our loved ones, our connections are cut. We are untethered. We are adrift and must find our way to a whole new self and a whole new world.

As you read our family's story, you will better understand the arduous journey we have been forced to take.

This book does not offer you psychological principles about the inner workings of grief, nor will you find a lengthy theological treatise on "Where is God when it hurts?" or "Why does a loving God allow suffering?" (as important as it is to explore those subjects). This book offers honest, hope-filled guidance from one griever to another.

This is the hardest of journeys. It's a journey no one would ever choose to make. A journey we would, if possible, avoid at all cost. Sadly, that is not an option. Although we are all "escape artists," accomplished at avoiding pain, the path of loss and sorrow allows no detours, no shortcuts, no workarounds. There is only one way, and that is *through*. But how? What does that even mean? I can only show you and tell you my experiences along the way, pointing out mistakes, dangers, and miracles.

My purpose in writing our story now is not to elicit pity or rekindle sorrow for you, my reader, but to give hope. It is my aim to remind those of you in your own darkest days that God is good. Through my struggles, I have found that God is still telling a good story with our lives—including yours. He stands between the pages of our lives and is leading us to a new place He is preparing.

God is not finished with our children's stories, He is not finished with our stories, and He is not finished with His own story. His story is about newness and life. He has planned a happy ending. In spite of everything, our God is still telling a good story with our lives, for He can do nothing less.

My heartfelt hope in sharing the thoughts in this book are echoed by the writer and poet Julia Cameron:

> I wish I could take language,
> And fold it like cool, moist rags,
> I would lay words on your forehead.
> I would wrap words on your wrists.
> "There, there," my words would say—
> Or something better.
> I would ask them to murmur,
> "Hush" and "Shh, shhh, it's all right."
> I would ask them to hold you all night.[1]

Prayer for Today

Lord, may the words within these pages speak peace and comfort to all who read them. In the name of Jesus, I pray. Amen.

PART ONE

Shattered

CHAPTER ONE

Brokenness:
The Struggle to Go On

"I am weary with my sighing; Every night I make
my bed swim, I flood my couch with my tears. My
eye has wasted away with grief."

— Psalm 6:6–7a

SONG TO HEAL YOUR HEART

"Scars in Heaven" by Casting Crowns

Austin

Strolling through the nursery, I pause, looking around at the
rose bushes. So many colors.

Images overwhelm me as I recall my daughter carrying a
beautiful bouquet of blush-colored roses down the church aisle
only four months earlier. Her image is overshadowed by another
of our young son's casket, laden with coral roses, being carried
down the church aisle a month ago.

Frozen in time and tearless, I stand there. *Strange*, I think, *how beauty triggers grief.* Sometimes sorrow wells up when I see blond children or a barefoot boy with long blond hair walking on the beach, surfboard in hand. Sometimes the emotion comes when seeing old people, for our boy will never grow old. Today, I have learned, it can be a flower.

Lost in my reverie, I do not hear a man approach.

"How are you holding up?" he asks.

Looking up from the plant that held me transfixed, I gaze with blank eyes into the face of an old friend. He was my philosophy teacher in college and taught a Sunday school class I attended a few times. He lost his wife two years earlier after her valiant battle with cancer.

"I'm okay," I stammer. "Doing pretty well. I think. I guess."

"Sometimes even those of us who know the Lord can lose our way, Cheryl. Grief does strange things."

What had he heard? I wonder but don't ask. *Were people talking about me? Could they see inside of me with a casual gaze?*

Of course, that's what I am—lost. I stand alone in crowds. There is no floor beneath me, no walls for support. There is no ceiling above my head. There is no hand to guide me. Even on this day filled with sunshine and warm breezes, I walk alone and aimless in darkness, knowing all the while the Lord waits near, longing to be present to me. I won't allow it—not yet.

How do I respond to my old friend, I wonder? Words have lost their meaning. Death silences.

Finally, he pats my arm and turns, walking away.

Soon, sitting in my car, my mind turns to a beautiful spring day in early May, seventeen years earlier.

My five-year-old daughter plays at my feet. It's almost three in the afternoon.

"The boys will be home from school soon, Mol," I murmur.

Our two boys always rode their bikes home from the elementary school just around the corner.

Picking up the ringing telephone, I thought of the coming year when Molly would start school. My daytime life would take on a new freedom that I hadn't known in a decade—no preschoolers at home.

"Congratulations, Cheryl," my doctor's happy voice announced. "You're going to have another baby."

Austin's life itself was a shock. At the time, we had three great kids—Wes, ten; Monty, nine; and Molly, five.

At first, we weren't delighted. It seemed like such an inconvenient time for another child. Many friends and some family members suggested abortion. It was never even a consideration. We knew we would manage. Most importantly, we believed then—and believe even more strongly now—that life is sacred.

Austin was a special addition to our family with his blond hair, hazel eyes, and just the right amount of freckles sprinkled across his nose. He was such a contrast to our three brown-eyed brunettes. In a day's time, we could not have imagined life without him. We were all in love with that little boy, who soon became the star of our family. We loved everything about him—his smiles, laughter, and antics. As he grew older, our family members adored him even more.

From an early age, Austin was a phenomenon on the basketball court. When he was in elementary school, the coach of the private school stopped us after a little dribbler game.

"If Austin will come to my school, I'll buy him a new bike and get him a charge account at McDonald's."

We laughed. But he said, "I'm really not kidding."

"Big A" became one of Austin's nicknames, even though he was not large or tall for his age. He excelled at all sports that he tried. Once in a Little League baseball game, he made a triple play. A father in the stands said to me, "You know what I like about him? He *thinks*."

Many of our friends had started homeschooling. Although it did not fit with our lifestyle, we decided to try homeschooling Austin in the fourth grade. Austin hated school. Our homeschool effort lasted only until Thanksgiving of that year. He desperately wanted to go back to school. His third-grade class had moved to another campus for fourth and fifth grade. Picking him up after school that first day, he was followed to our car by a posse of kids who had taken to him, like a celebrity trailed by fans. He was always a magnet for others.

When Austin was in middle school, we sold our family home where we had raised our children for over twenty years. Our three older children were finishing college and starting to marry. Austin had attended public and private schools, and we were again searching for the best school situation for this lively, funny fourteen-year-old boy of ours. We had been considering a move to a smaller golf course community outside of town. My husband had always wanted to live on a golf course. I was not on board with the move. But there was still turbulence in our local schools due to our area's late compliance with desegregation laws. Austin received a knife threat on the last day of sixth grade. That cinched the move for me. The new school was ranked high scholastically and had a renowned basketball program.

Gary and I had worked in his parents' photography business after we married and had purchased it from them years before the move. I didn't like the fact that work was so far from what

A Portrait of Grief

would be our new home and down a dangerous highway, but the advantages seemed to outweigh the disadvantages.

We leased a house in the new community while beginning to build a smaller dream home. The old rental house we leased was painted red and smelled dank inside. Austin quickly dubbed it "The Barn."

After moving into The Barn, I felt a strange lull in my life. I realized that I was content in that ugly old house. What I loved so deeply were the people inside.

It was a time of new beginnings—a new community, a new house, a new season with kids moving on. In the few years before, sadly, I had buried both my parents. I knew they were safe with the Lord. Relieved of caregiving duties, the future looked bright and hopeful.

It was a time of special closeness to the Lord for me. In those days of contentment, writing in my journal, setting my goals for the years ahead, I asked my God, who knows the future, to "choose for me." I had begun to pray, "You choose Lord. Choose your best for me." It was my way of surrendering my will to His will.

Then came the flood, and then came death.

It began with a combination of meteorological events hovering over Hardin and Jefferson counties that dropped thirty inches of rain in a thirty-hour period. The flooding was widespread, complicated by rising water from the Pine Island Bayou and other waterways. Both the house we were leasing and the house we were building were flooded with over three feet of water. We were rescued by friends and waited for the floodwaters to subside. We pulled our treasures out of the mud, picked through anything we could salvage, and threw away the rest. It was a huge loss. Most people in the area had one house flooded. We had two.

We said goodbye to The Barn and rented yet another house in town, moving what furniture that survived. We continued building our dream home after the waters subsided.

Finally, Gary, Austin, and I moved into our new home—not knowing that we would have less than two years together.

It wasn't easy working in town twenty minutes from our home. Our life was already complicated by the givens of a life in photography. We often worked late into the night and on weekends. Our support group dwindled with the move, and I was aware that Austin was left alone far too much. He had started driving and was traveling the same dangerous road that we traveled to work.

In our new home, I looked through the dining room window. I had taken a nap, preparing for the late night ahead photographing a wedding. I watched as Austin climbed into the Pickle (Austin's name for my green car) with his friend and drove away as I breathed a prayer, "Please protect him, Lord."

We arrived home late that night after sending off our bride and groom through hundreds of flashes. As we prepared for bed, at 11:45 p.m., three of Austin's friends came to our front door. The boys were visibly shaken.

One of them spoke up with a quavering voice. "Mr., Mrs. Christopher, there's been an accident... it's bad... Austin... they have the jaws of life. We couldn't stand for you not to know."

A patrolman arrived at our driveway just as we were running out to our car to hurry to the accident site. The officer leaped from his car and rushed toward us. He said the words every parent dreads: "Mr. Christopher, Mrs. Christopher, I regret to inform you that your son, Austin, has been pronounced dead at the scene of an accident."

I fell to the ground. Picking me up, Gary carried me into the house. He called friends to stay with me while he went to the scene with the officer.

Austin's group of friends had met for pizza in Beaumont. Austin had left my car at a friend's house to ride with others. An older boy who Austin did not know very well begged Austin to ride home with him. On the way home, the boy tried to pass one of their friends in another car. The friend challenged their speed, would not let them pass, and the race was on.

Somehow, the cars touched, throwing our boy's car off the highway and into a tree. The car must somehow have gone airborne since it hit the tree twelve feet above the ground. The driver of Austin's car was thrown from the vehicle and, though badly injured, lived. No one in the second car was injured. Only our boy, with his seat belt on, had been killed.

For several hours after we were notified of our son's death, I would not speak to God and would not allow anyone in my presence to speak to Him. The pastor who lived next door had come over and wanted to pray with me. "No," I stopped him. "I'm not speaking to God, and I don't want you to either in my presence. Go in the other room and pray for the boy who was driving and is still alive."

Though I would not speak to Him, the Lord continued to speak to my heart. First, when I went into my bedroom alone, I heard His gentle words, "Don't push me away, Cheryl. I know how it feels to lose a son. I still have plans for Austin, your family, for you."

Breaking my silence, I demanded, "This is it? This is what You've chosen for me? This is Your best?"

In our horror and heartbreak, we were surrounded by the love of God through His people. Our every need was provided. But we had been broken. Suffering became our norm. All the music went out of our lives.

CHAPTER TWO

Anguish: An Encounter with Terror

"You will not be afraid of the terror by night,
Or the arrow that flies by day;
Of the plague that stalks in darkness,
Or of the destruction that devastates at noon."

— Psalm 91:5–6

SONG TO HEAL YOUR HEART

"It Is Well"—Kristene DiMarco | You Make Me Brave

Wes: Nine Years Later

On a clear and beautiful April evening, we received a phone call from our daughter.

Gary answered the phone.

"Dad," she said, "I got a weird text from Wes. He sent it before five o'clock, but I just noticed it. It says, 'I'm so sorry.' I think something's wrong."

My husband called our oldest son. When Wes didn't answer, he called our daughter-in-law. I could only hear my husband's side of the conversation. I heard him say, "He—he did what?"

Turning to me, speaking quietly, he said, "Wes shot himself. He's dead."

Our son Monty arrived at our home almost immediately after we got the call. I was still screaming. Friends Linda and Brad Brock came in with him. I was frenzied, with my mouth still open in a scream—a scream that never came, or has it already? I don't know. It is a soundless scream—the scream of one with no more tears to cry and yet with horror that would not stop. I ran out the front door and kept running, my mouth in the frozen scream. My friend Mary Milligan came from somewhere, ran after me in the dark, caught me, found my shoes, and walked me home.

"No one can look at me," I told her over and over again. She helped me change into a nightgown and tucked me into bed. I vaguely remember people appearing at the bedside during the evening, but it is all a blurry fog. I couldn't feel anything and stayed in bed until our daughter arrived sometime the following day and forced me out of bed.

Wes had sat down, written letters to his father, brother, sister, wife, his three boys, and to me. He laid out all his keys, his insurance policy, his pertinent business papers to make things easier on everyone and then took his life—knowing he would be received on the other side by his God. (Wes made a decision to receive Christ at an early age and was confident in that, as were we.) He just did not see any way out of his problems. He thought it was an unselfish act and thought he was doing us all a favor.

He was wrong.

Our oldest child, Wes, was good at everything he tried. He had a photographic memory and found school to be an easy undertaking. With our son Monty being only fourteen months younger, they were sports competitors and best friends.

The boys looked like twins, and I often dressed them alike. They were a team. Some of our friends' kids called them MontyWes. If I could have named their team, I would have named it Trouble. They were always making some.

It was hard to leave them with a babysitter to run to work to help with a portrait. I would return home to find that my three and four-year-old boys had escaped out of the front window. One of their sitters resigned after the first day. The boys had cornered her, pulled down their pants, and took aim, threatening to wet her if she interfered with their play any longer.

At the mall, they pulled the shoes from a display, disappeared beneath the clothes, and took a swim in the fountain. I reluctantly decided it was best for me to stay at home for many years.

Wes's first word was *ball*, and with superb hand-eye coordination, he was a superstar in Little League. Even as a child, his energy level was high, and he was always on the go. Further, Wes liked to be prepared. The night before his first day in school, I went into his room to tuck him in and discovered him fully dressed for school, lying on his side with his backpack on his back.

In high school, Wes was a ranked tennis player before he decided to switch from tennis to golf before his junior year. He played golf for the high school team during his junior and senior years. Wes was offered and refused a full golf scholarship to our local university, Lamar, because his heart was set on Texas A&M University.

He attended A&M for two years while continuing to work on his golf game. Wes placed third in the Texas Collegiate at Waterwood and was asked to join the LSU college golf team by a coach that had been following his progress. It didn't take Wes long to transfer his loyalty to the purple and gold, even sporting a tiger tattoo on his rear-end to prove his love for the Tigers.

Although usually upbeat and energetic, Wes did have a sensitive side. The first evidence that I remember of depression in Wes's life showed itself after a broken engagement. He had met a darling girl in Beaumont, soon bringing her home for us to meet. In time, he asked for our blessing on their engagement.

We arranged for them to go to a spiritual marriage retreat sponsored by Focus on the Family, hoping to ensure a strong union. To our sorrow and his, that love ended with her breaking the engagement and telling him she had aborted his child. Wes was crushed. I went to San Antonio, where he was living to stay with him. Devastated, he always remembered that lost child.

Wes worked for his two uncles, who owned a medical supply company. When his uncles, my husband's brothers, had a falling out that led to lawsuits, Wes felt divided loyalties and left the job. He came home to work with us for a while in the photography business. It was during this time that he met his future bride in Beaumont.

They dated for about three months before marrying and leaving Beaumont. There was some volatility in their relationship, but we prayed for God's blessings.

Within several years, it was obvious that Wes was also a leader in business. He headed the Houston office for a new business in employee leasing. He also managed their sales statewide. Wes was a closer. He would be called in to close all the big deals. He had reached a pinnacle in golf, playing in two US

A Portrait of Grief

Mid-Amateurs and the US and British Amateur. He was the 2002 Harmon Champion in Houston.

Wes never met a stranger and had many loyal friends. Wes loved learning new things, eating new foods, and playing with his boys.

Despite success in many areas, Wes had a troubled marriage. After three sons, their relationship was unraveling. They had separated in the fall of the year but were trying again. Somehow things spiraled out of control.

In the midst of this downward spiral, the call came to our home that Wes ended his life.

CHAPTER THREE

Heartbreak: Surviving Sorrow and Travail

"The Lord is near to the brokenhearted And saves those who are crushed in spirit."

— Psalm 34:18

SONG TO HEAL YOUR HEART

"You're Still God" by Philippa Hanna

Brock: Thirteen Years Later

After Wes's death, we sold our business and moved to the Texas Hill Country, living there for ten years. During that time, I began oil painting.

In April 2018, Gary was on a golf trip; I was at home painting a landscape.

I felt a hand on my shoulder—it frightened me. There was no one around. The hand was warm and comforting. Peace engulfed me.

"Is that You, Lord?" I stammered.

Trembling, I sat down in wonder. "What is it? Is something going to happen? If You want me to know something, You've got to tell me!"

Opening my Bible, it fell open to Ecclesiastes.

A good name is better than a precious perfume, and the day of one's death better than the day of one's birth. It is better to go to the house of mourning than to the house of feasting, for that [the day of death] is the end of every man, and the living will take it to heart and solemnly ponder its meaning. Sorrow is better than laughter.

— Ecclesiastes 7:1–3a (AMP)

Brock, our oldest grandson, had trouble fitting in at school and struggled at home. He was Wes's oldest son and was eight years old when his father died.

As a child, Brock had an incredible faith in God. When my husband told him of his dad's death, he cried, "No, no! We've got to pray. We've got to pray." He bowed his head and led all the adults in a prayer for his dad, for his brothers, and for himself. The room was filled with amazing grace.

Brock had a great heart. He was twelve when hurricane Matthew hit Haiti and Brock went door to door collecting money to aid the Haitians. Adding all his own savings to the pile, he sent it to the relief fund. After hearing they had no drinking water, he refused to take baths or showers until it was absolutely demanded.

Brock was an unusually beautiful child and a handsome young man with a captivating voice well suited to radio. Talented in drawing, he also loved to cook. He had a sensitive spirit that made his life—with its family troubles—even more difficult.

Three years after his father's death, Brock's mother remarried. Soon afterward, Brock started cutting himself. We were appalled and at a loss to know how to help with this destructive act of self-harm. We could find little information at that time to explain his desperation. His mother took him to a psychiatrist, who diagnosed Brock with ADHD and depression. The remarriage lasted only for eighteen months before dissolving into divorce. Brock continued to struggle.

Following the divorce, the ex-husband started filing lawsuits over dissatisfaction with the divorce settlement. After a five-year period of litigation, attorneys had most of the money Wes had left for his family.

This was a hard time for everyone. The home life was always in turmoil. It seemed Brock could do nothing right, and he got the brunt of the punishment. Later we discovered he was being put out of the house and on the street overnight for punishment.

When Brock was older and had a phone, he often called us to come and get him. We did. He lived with us off and on from the time he was fourteen. Still, his great desire was always to go back home. He bounced around a lot, back and forth between his mother and us.

The last time Brock lived with us began in the summer after his junior year in high school. In a short time, it became obvious he was trying to fill an empty spot inside with alcohol and pills. I caught him huffing something from the garage in a brown paper bag and discovered empty vodka bottles hidden in shoeboxes in the closet.

We talked to him, prayed with him and for him. We took him to counselors, we took him to church, sent him to Young Life Camp, and tried to get him involved in spiritual things. Our Young Life friends, John and Debbie Wayland, took him to Disney World with their family while we were on a prescheduled trip to Europe.

We were out of our depth with Brock. Looking back, I'm afraid he manipulated us badly.

In his senior year, he begged us to let him go home to Houston for Christmas. Since his mother was willing, he went the 197 miles by an express bus, intending to stay just a few days. He tried to take his own life while there, one of many attempts.

He went into counseling in Houston and, when released, was planning to come back to us. We were told the psychologists wanted to know why he was living with us when he had abandonment issues with his mom. He and his mother decided for him to stay at home. When talking on the phone about his decision to stay, he told me, "I've got to try again." Brock loved his family and always wanted to go back home. He was always hopeful that things would be different. Later, we discovered the last few months of his senior year were in a homeless shelter for teens.

With the help of a high school principal and a coach, Brock secured a scholarship to Houston Baptist University and spent a year there. It was not a successful year for him. He went home for Easter and again attempted suicide.

The last time he stayed with us, I awoke at 3 a.m. to find him in the kitchen getting a beer. I tried to talk to him, but it was obvious that he had taken something. "Just a minute, just a minute," he kept saying.

I followed him out to the little casita just outside our main house, where guests stay. There he had a row of pills carefully laid out, ready to take. He only said, "Promise you won't tell Grandad."

I scooped up all the pills that I could find and put him to bed. At last, back in bed, I laid awake crying and praying until daylight.

My husband and I talked the next morning. We decided we couldn't continue to do this. He needed more help than we were equipped to give. We were at the end of our rope. When Brock got up, we told him he couldn't stay any longer, that he had to go into rehab.

"You can't die here," I told him.

We begged him to let us place him in rehab. We promised to help him put his life back together, but he must get clean. He refused, and because he was nineteen, we couldn't force him.

We agreed to drive him to Houston to the homeless center Covenant House, which was his choice.

I cried all the way there and back, unable to believe we were leaving our grandson in a homeless situation.

The following week, with his mother's help, he did go into rehab. He wrote a beautiful letter to us from the rehab telling us that he had burned all his bridges and was going to get better. We desperately hoped he would. The stress had done something to me, and I came down with shingles. I knew I couldn't control Brock, his decisions, or his safety.

That Christmas, we spent time with Brock and his brothers in Houston. He was out of rehab, living in a halfway house, working, and appeared to be doing well.

It didn't last long. He went from rehab to rehab. We couldn't keep up with him during those months since rehab facilities routinely confiscated his phone.

Looking back on the night I was painting, and the passage to Ecclesiastes came to me, I think the Lord simply wanted to assure me before the fact that He knew the future, that He was still in control, for it was only hours before Brock took his life.

After the call came, I knew not to call any of the family to share the news. It was late. I had learned that tragedy is best heard in the morning. There was nothing they could do.

Since I was alone, I got into bed with my little poodle and lay there, willing my heart to stop pounding.

"Do people die of a broken heart?" I asked the Lord.

PART TWO

Healing

CHAPTER FOUR

Grief and Mourning: What's Happening?

"For our momentary, light affliction is producing for us an eternal weight of glory far beyond all comparison, while we look not at the things which are seen, but at the things which are not seen; for the things which are seen are temporal, but the things which are not seen are eternal."

— 2 Corinthians 4:17–18

SONG TO HEAL YOUR HEART

"Trust in You" by Lauren Daigle

In the beginning, in the acute state of grief, you may wonder, *What's happening to me?*

Shock and disorientation are common first experiences. You may feel confused, numb, overwhelmed, and in despair. You may feel nothing. Your mind may go blank. Everyone is different. Whatever you are feeling, know that it is not constant but will ebb and flow into other feelings.

Grief is what you think and feel on the inside after the tragic loss of a loved one. Mourning, or lamentation, describes the outward expression of those feelings. Crying, sadness, wailing, despair, yearning, hurt, and anguish are examples of mourning behavior.

Grief and mourning encompass the process of coping, which we must experience in working through a traumatic loss. It can last a long time. The process involves many different emotions, actions, and expressions. It is an undertaking that helps us, in time, to reach a degree of acceptance.

Whose job is it to teach us about grief and mourning? I was at a complete loss when the time came. When faced with sorrow, disappointments, or hurt feelings in the past, I was accustomed to dealing with the emotions inside and in private. But with the loss of a child, this was too big, too explosive to contain. There was a howl inside of me that frightened me. What would happen if I let it out? I tiptoed across the surface of my feelings, afraid to let go, afraid of falling into a pit of despair that had no bottom. There was a profound uncertainty within me, wondering if survival was even possible.

It took a long time to understand the importance of mourning. It seemed to hurt so much more when my feelings were allowed to escape from inside to the outside where I could see and hear them—where others could see them and hear them.

There emerged within me an independent streak that demanded holding my feelings inside, holding my encouragers at a distance. I would not become a wounded bird, protected beneath the wings of others! I would be strong! The problem with that resolve is that I didn't know what "being strong" meant in this situation. It seemed right to attempt to avoid the pain, to seal it off as best I could. After all, it was my long-established technique for dealing with loss.

After the loss of our boys, our home was filled with so many people, and we were surrounded by distraction for the first weeks. But there comes a time when there is no distraction strong enough to deny the reality and the emotions that accompany it, no matter the amount of determination. When unable to keep the emotions inside, I would go to my room, where I could be alone to cry or scream. Emerging from my room, courageous expression in place, with a calm demeanor, I could tell others had heard my despair by the silence that greeted me.

Appearances matter in America. Our society is uncomfortable with death and mourning. Grievers are treated differently. We are awkward and make others uncomfortable. Even close friends may shy away from visiting and hesitate to say our lost loved one's name. We attempt to shroud death with silence and conceal it with flowers.

With our loved ones freshly in the ground, we were encouraged to watch a funny movie or go out to dinner. Although no one encourages it, death must be acknowledged, not denied. Death is not diminished through denial but grows ever more frightening.

It is a paradox. In relinquishing control, in unleashing our reserves, some amount of relief can be experienced. Although no one is comfortable with unbridled emotions, this is not a time for repression!

I am not saying we can be in control of our grief and mourning. We don't really "do" grief; it "does" us. Grief picks us up and moves us to a place we've never been before. In the beginning, we can't really talk about what we are feeling because we don't know what we feel. Feelings rise up from some unknown place in the most unexpected ways and times. Feelings recede and fade only to be resurrected in quiet moments. The best we can do is to go with it. It's like riding a wave instead of standing still as it hits.

In my ignorance of the process, I silenced my mourning, and the grief invaded my dreams, catching me up in terrifying, irrational, and smoky scenes of desperate attempts to rescue my son, who lies trapped in a car. Dreams seem to be a way for our unconscious mind to work out terrors our conscious mind cannot face.

"She is still herself," I heard people whisper. "She's going to be okay. She can still laugh."

But I was *not* okay. I was inconsolable. With Bonhoeffer, we wonder, "Who am I? Are we what others see, or are we what we know of ourselves? Restless and longing and sick."

I would never be the same person, for I now knew a truth I had only been told about in stories. I now knew that children could die—that my child could die. I thought I could imagine what a parent would feel when losing a child, but I was wrong. There is no way to imagine such a thing. This was shocking beyond my imagination.

I have learned, finally, that the mourning is important and not to be avoided. Don't cover up, don't deny, don't protect others by sealing yourself inside. Don't anesthetize the pain with alcohol or pills. The only way to healing is through engaging in the mourning process. While there is no obvious right or wrong way to grieve, it is best to let it happen. Feel the feelings and let them flow out. Don't hide the despair, and don't worry about the reaction of others. Don't deny your emotions or bottle them up. The pain will never go away until it is experienced again and again and again.

A Portrait of Grief

As much as I wish it were otherwise, there are no secret formulas to get us through the pain of grief and the mourning for our dearest loves. We must each forge our own path, which is like hiking up a steep mountain in the fog.

In Hannah Hurnard's allegorical classic *Hinds Feet on High Places*, the author describes a new believer, Much-Afraid, as she starts on her journey to the High Places with the Lord Shepherd. The Shepherd introduces Much-Afraid to her traveling guides, Sorrow and her twin sister, Suffering:

> I cannot go with them, she gasped. I can't! I can't! Oh My Lord Shepherd, why do you do this to me? How can I travel in their company? It is more than I can bear. You tell me the mountain way itself is so steep and difficult that I cannot climb it alone. Then why, oh why, must you make Sorrow and Suffering my companions? Couldn't you have given Joy and Peace to go with me to strengthen me and encourage me on the difficult way? I never thought you would do this to me!
>
> The Shepherd answered, "you remember your promise, to accept the helpers that I would give, because you believed that I would choose the very best possible guides for you. Will you still trust me, Much Afraid?"[2]

I don't claim to understand the Lord's dealings with His children in allowing tragic events that alter the very meaning and direction of our lives. I don't know what to attribute to

God's will and what to blame on Satan. In reading Job, it is clear there is more at play that we know.

The author Buel Kazee says that when a Christian makes a real surrender,

> He is now in the land of the Giants. Instead of expecting ease and comfort, now he must expect war. He is no longer a babe in Christ, but a soldier of the Cross... He is now in the land where the battle is against 'spiritual wickedness in high places and the weapons of our warfare are not carnal, but spiritual. It is the 'good fight of faith,' and we are to have our faith tested at every round. It is a walk now from one situation to another, with opposition at every turn. Lions' dens and fiery furnaces and Goliaths will be ever in our pathway. [3]

It is a fight of faith, for that is what the enemy is seeking to destroy—our faith.

Yet, we have no strength for fighting. I know the Lord sends more than the twins Sorrow and Suffering to help us on the way. He comes Himself. The Lord promises to stay close to us:

> "Do not fear, for I am with you; Do not be afraid, for I am your God. I will strengthen you, I will also help you, I will also uphold you with my righteous right hand."

> — Isaiah 41:10

We must remember His promises now in the worst of times. Although it is important to feel our feelings, we must not trust them. Feelings and emotions are just that, feelings and emotions. They don't always speak the truth. Grief makes us pretty much crazy people. You can't really trust yourself while in grief. That's why we are advised to wait a year before making any significant decisions.

Just because we don't "feel" very spiritual at the time doesn't negate who we are: God's children. Just because we don't "feel" God's presence does not mean He is not present in our lives. Just because we can't see a future doesn't mean there isn't one. These are the days to hold to the truth. These are the days to hold to our faith.

In Thessalonians 4:13, the Apostle Paul says, "But we do not want you to be uninformed, brethren, about those who are asleep, so that you may not grieve as the rest who have no hope."

Paul doesn't say that you may not grieve, but that you may not grieve as others do who have no hope.

Death is real, and it is right for believers to grieve and mourn. We have lost our children, a part of ourselves—maybe the most important part. We don't protect God's reputation by denying or suppressing our feelings as I did. He is big enough to take care of Himself. Our God is not afraid of our tears. He is not shocked by our behavior. He knows us and has chosen to love us anyway.

But the hope is real too. In these days of forgetfulness, we must remember to hold to our promised hope of reunion.

In this process of mourning, it seems we are going nowhere. If anything, we are moving backward. It is truly a path filled with stumbling steps forward, staggering steps back, circles, and stops. But slowly, ever so slowly, you will move forward. You won't see the progress—like much of life; it becomes visible only as we look back.

When I worked in France, I learned to speak a little more French than I did in my high school French classes. I love their word for our English word *goodbye*. It is *au-revoir*. It means "until we meet again."

I must trust God's Word that death is not goodbye but just an au-revoir.

Prayer for Today

Oh Lord, today I feel so hopeless, so faithless. Fill me with Your Spirit of love, for I desire to be hopeful. Strengthen me, for I desire to be faithful. Assure me of Your compassionate care for my child in his last moments on earth. Whisper the words of life and resurrection to me again and again. These things I ask in the name of Your son, Your only son. Amen.

CHAPTER FIVE

Denial and Avoidance: This Can't Be Happening

"Beloved, do not be surprised at the fiery ordeal among you, which comes upon you for your testing, as though something strange were happening to you."

— 1 Peter 4:12

SONG TO HEAL YOUR HEART

"I Will Stand by You" by Rascal Flatts

The Bible is filled with the suffering of God's people from cover to cover.

As Paul David Tripp points out in his book *Suffering*,

The Bible never presents suffering as an idea or a concept but puts it before us in the blood-and-guts drama of real human experiences. When it comes to suffering, Scripture is never avoidant or cosmetic in its approach. The Bible never minimizes the harsh experience of life in this terribly broken world, and in doing so, the Bible forces us out of our denial and toward humble honesty.[4]

We must strive to be honest about what has happened, for the loss of a child changes everything. The meaning is drained from our lives. Direction and structure evaporate when there is no meaning. After losing a child, we realize that we lost not only that child but also our assumptive world—our beliefs about what the world should be like. It is little wonder then that the death of a child at any age creates in us a struggle to make sense of the world. We must have an honest appraisal of ourselves, who we were, and who we want to become—for there is no going back.

Facing the future honestly is a part of the first work of grief.

Refusing to face facts for a long period of time is unhealthy. Sometimes, though, a short period of denial can be helpful. Denial doesn't feel like an attitude that you choose, rather one that emerges. Being in denial can give your mind the opportunity to unconsciously absorb shocking or distressing information at a pace that won't send you into a tailspin.

After a traumatic event, you might need several days or weeks to process what has happened and come to grips with the challenges ahead. We must not linger too long in denial. In the words of Ernest Becker's *The Denial of Death,* "We must take care not to tranquilize {ourselves} with the trivial." We must not use drinking and drugging, sex, or even shopping to anesthetize ourselves.

I have had to make peace with some of the choices I made in the traumatic early days that I would now change if I could. I did not go to the scene of Austin's accident. It was only a mile from

A Portrait of Grief

our home, but I just couldn't go. Fear of seeing him crushed or broken overwhelmed me. I wish now that I had gone.

We did go to the funeral home and sit with him before the day of the funeral. The funeral director counseled us strongly to have the casket open during the funeral. I did not want that. It felt like people would be looking at him in his sleep. It seemed an invasion of his privacy. I also wanted the focus on the hope of resurrection, not the sorrow of death. I did allow the casket to be open until right before the family was entering the door of the church. The director had finally convinced me it was important for all the grieving kids to see him and grasp the reality of early death.

My husband allowed me to make all these decisions, for which I am very grateful. He allowed me to plan the funeral, choose the music, select the photographs.

After the death of our oldest son, Wes, we never saw him. After the first call, we could not locate his wife. She had her cell phone disconnected. When our boy's body was released, my husband brought him home from Houston.

Again, as with Austin, we received friends in our home. We never went to be with Wes or to see him. We were all shocked and in shock at what had happened and feared what we would see since he died of a gunshot. I regret that cowardice.

Wes's children were so confused by all that was happening. They were young, and my husband tried to explain, telling them their dad died in an accident. With us all in shock, I know it was unclear and confusing. I heard Wes's middle son, Carson, who was six, ask as we were leaving the church and the casket was being hoisted by the pallbearers, "Is Dad in that box?"

We did not view our grandson, Brock, either. We didn't even know where he was taken, nor did I ask. His mother was in charge then, and we had little say in his final care. We did arrange the funeral and called our good friend and Young Life leader, John Wayland, who had come when we lost Austin, Wes, and now Brock, to again speak words of hope. We paid the expenses of the funeral with money Brock had earned while living with us, and we were saving for him to buy a car. We owed him that.

Most parents I have spoken with find that they become more honest in their approach to life as time goes on. I certainly did. Author Larry Crabb says, "An aching soul is evidence not of neurosis or spiritual immaturity, but of realism."

I now regret not going to the scene of Austin's accident. I regret not going to Wes and holding him a last time. I regret not spending time at the side of our grandson, Brock, after his death. But at the time, I couldn't. I couldn't do it. Is that denial? Or is it self-protection? Some things are not possible for some people. I have had to make peace with my choices.

The question of our suffering is a calamity with no answers. We are like a crab whose shell has been shattered, for we have lost all the security we have built around ourselves. This is an in-between time filled with disappointment and despair.

The world as we knew it is gone forever. We wander around like zombies with no direction. Despair can cause us to lose our way. Many turn to the quick fixes of sex or new relationships, drugs, gambling, alcohol, busyness, or pornography. Today there are so many paths that lead away from health and wholeness that they can't all be listed. I would call this avoidance rather than denial.

In his book *Inside Out*, Larry Crabb tells the story of a man who has come to him for counseling. The man has an urgent request: "I want to feel better quick."

After pausing for a moment, Crabb then replied, "I suggest you get a case of your favorite alcoholic beverage, find some cooperative woman, and go to the Bahamas for a month."

Now it was the man's turn to pause. He stared at Dr. Crabb, looking puzzled, then asked, "Are you a Christian?"

"Why do you ask?"

"Well, your advice doesn't sound very biblical."

"It's the best I can do given your request. If you really want to feel good right away and get rid of any unpleasant emotion, then I don't recommend following Christ. Drunkenness, immoral pleasures, and vacations will work far better. Not for long, of course, but in the short run, they'll give you what you want."[5]

Many follow the road of quick fixes. They are beguiling. They help us change the subject from death to something, *anything* but the death of our children.

Scripture paints a portrait to those of us suffering of a God who understands, a God who cares. We are advised to go to Him for help. He promises to stick by us and one day to wipe away all our tears once and for all. While being totally honest about our suffering, the Bible lays out a path for us to follow. Move toward God, not away.

I looked back through my journal to the days leading up to the car accident where Austin died. I had written these verses:

- "For I am persuaded that neither death, nor life, nor angels, nor principalities, nor things present, nor things to come, nor powers, nor height, nor depth, nor any other thing, shall be able to separate us from the love of God, which is in Christ Jesus our Lord" (Romans 8:38–39, KJV).

- "Yea, though I walk through the valley of the shadow of death, I will fear no evil, for thou art with me" (Psalm 23:4).
- "Do not fear, for I am with you; Do not be afraid, for I am your God. I will strengthen you, surely I will help you. Surely, I will uphold you with my right hand" (Isaiah 41:10).

Again, I see the Lord is there, shoring up my faith ahead of my need while life was normal. And yet, I moved away from Him for a long time.

At church, I practiced wearing a totally blank face, with no joy and no sorrow. The truth is that blankness is a lie—it is the mask we often wear. The sorrow oozed from my pores; it escaped through my tearless eyes. I held my silence as a shield.

After one really bad day, I took a walk at about 6 p.m. in the evening. I told the Lord, "I need You to speak to me. I have nothing to say to You. I don't want to talk. I don't want to pray. Just speak to me."

As I walked and tried to keep my mind still and quiet, the voice of the Lord spoke inside my spirit. He whispered, "Trust me, Cheryl. Just trust me. I still have a plan, even in this."

I replied, "Don't think you can enlarge me through this, Lord. You watch me. I intend to get littler and littler! Don't You cause good to come from this, Lord! No good is good enough!"

And I did get littler. I rebelled against the sermons at church. The preacher had all the answers, three-point formulas, pithy phrases. Everything was so clear to him, so orderly, as he tucked his children in at night. He made life sound so simple, so confident in the reward for good living. That was not my experience.

The joyful praise music at our church sounded like a hootenanny to my broken heart. We left the church to attend a more formal church, where the formal, dirge-like music spoke to me in my sorrow.

Sometime in the second year of our first walk with sorrow, I insisted we put the beautiful green sofa, my tear-soaked grieving couch, out on the street. I just couldn't bear to look at it any longer.

Not everyone has that need. Some people have no problem going back to the church where they buried their children. Some can remain in their homes and take comfort there. I could not. There is no right or wrong in this. We learned to do what we needed to do (or perhaps I should say my husband listened to me and did what I needed).

After the first year, I knew I did not want to live in our house anymore. I begged Gary to put it on the market. It didn't sell.

Eight or nine months into that second year, Gary and I were sitting on the porch swing. The sun was setting, and he said, "Isn't that beautiful?"

I didn't respond.

He said angrily, "What's wrong with you? Can't you even enjoy a beautiful sunset anymore?"

"I don't want to be here. I don't want to live here."

"I love it here," he countered.

"We built this house for three people," I sobbed. "It will always be empty to me! I'll make you a deal; if the house doesn't sell in two more months (the end of the second year without Austin), I will find a way to live here and never mention it again."

Silently, I told the Lord, "Please send someone to buy this house. You've got two months."

The telephone in the house rang instantly.

"That's probably somebody wanting to buy this darn house," my husband muttered. And it was.

In the words of author Keith Wall, "Sometimes God just shows up."

Prayer for Today

Lord, even in my rebellion, You stay the same. I'm angry but awed. How can I contain such contradictory thoughts and feelings? How can You not walk away from me when I don't praise You? When I turn from You? Yet still, You answer my prayers.

Oh, I forgot. You love prodigals, don't You? I still believe, but I'm short on praise. Forgive me, for I know You are worthy. Amen.

CHAPTER SIX

The Stages: And the Worst They Have to Offer

"After you have suffered for a little while, the God of all grace, who called you to His eternal glory in Christ, will Himself perfect, confirm, strengthen and establish you."

— 1 Peter 5:10

SONG TO HEAL YOUR HEART

"Spirit Lead Me" by Influence Music and Michael Ketterer

The symptoms and stages of grief have been well chronicled, popularized by Dr. Elisabeth Kubler-Ross's 1969 book *On Death and Dying*. The five grief stages—commonly recognized as denial, anger, bargaining, depression, and acceptance—were identified through Kubler-Ross's work with terminally ill patients and not with those left behind to grieve. The Kubler-Ross model, while not complete, is helpful in providing a framework and context for those suddenly plunged into grief. Without some context, most people would be in a cauldron of confusion, wondering what in the world they're going through.

Acute mourning can, however, involve many more and different stages than the ones she recognized.

It is often said that the normal grief process is difficult and messy. I don't believe there *is* a "normal" grief process. That's the problem. If only we could say, "Okay, I've passed through denial, and now it's on to anger. Just three more stages and I will be back to normal!"

But that's not how it is. We don't follow stages—we jump around from one moment to the next, from one day to the next. And each of us experiences grief uniquely and personally. We might have previously imagined what it would be like to suffer deep loss but then most likely be entirely shocked by the actual experience. We may have experienced grief from an earlier loss, and when faced with a second loss, we encounter an entirely new experience.

Believers in God and His sovereign will truly desire to trust and honor Him in bad times. However, we might be surprised at our actions and reactions in our helpless state. In fact, even the strongest of believers may discover they act in unexpected, unimagined ways.

Some symptoms I experienced and others have spoken to me about include:

- Denial
- Repetitive or frightening dreams
- Flashbacks
- Fantasy
- Sleep disorders
- Confusion and indecisiveness
- Shock

A Portrait of Grief

- Depression
- Yearning
- Hyperactivity
- Seeking reconnection to the deceased person
- Bitterness
- Anxiety or Panic attacks
- Meaninglessness
- Hostility
- Irritability
- Numbness
- Anger
- Overeating
- Under-eating
- Excessive drinking
- Sexual encounters
- Hopelessness
- Guilt
- Obsessive preoccupation with the events
- Impatience
- Pornography
- Powerlessness
- Extravagant shopping
- Flashbacks
- Physical illness
- Controlling behavior
- Fear
- Loss of energy
- Crying
- Wailing
- Suicidal thoughts
- Selfishness

I have come to believe that grief, above all, is essentially about love. It is love that has lost its recipient. As Claudio Gray says, "Now I know that grief is a whetstone that sharpens all you love, all your happiest memories, into blades that tear you apart from within."[6]

It is important to point out that our emotions are not wrong or sinful. We may feel uncomfortable or even ashamed because of "negative" emotions such as rage, resentment, or bitterness. But these feelings need not be classified or categorized, and it doesn't help to label them as "bad" or "good." They are emotions, which occur naturally because we are human and because we have suffered heartache.

At times of great loss, and as already stated, we must let our emotions wash over us. God holds us accountable for our actions, not our feelings. Our emotions are a healthy and gracious gift from God. In grief, we must not stifle them, though sometimes we must learn to control how they are expressed.

After being informed of our son Austin's death, wrapped in a blanket of shock, I sat on the green couch in our small library. Turning to my friend Linda sitting beside me, I commented, "I feel like I'm waiting for something."

She responded, "You are. You're waiting for time to pass."

In death, everything comes to a standstill. It is as though time is frozen. Grieving is marked by a lag—everything stops. Waiting for time to pass, I sat and waited, feeling empty and vacant.

This was most likely numbness, some denial, and a little shock thrown in as well. At the first jolt of loss, experiences and conversations can be blurred or hazy. You may not yet feel any of the deep feelings of grief. People in shock often appear to be behaving normally without a lot of emotion because the news hasn't fully sunk in.

Numbness is a natural protection when facing any kind of trauma. Detached from the reality of the loss, you may be able to function pretty well at first. This can be confusing to the people around you when they expect full-blown grief and suffering that you don't yet feel.

Some people I've spoken with feel they are spinning out of control. It is normal to want order and predictability. I have said we are crazy people, and we are. Often obsessed with details of our loss, sleep-deprived, and confused. Although it may feel as though you have lost your mind, you have not. You may be driving and not remember where you are going. You may lose your phone, your keys, your wallet, or your purse. You may forget appointments, forget the dog at the groomer, or walk from room to room looking for some forgotten item.

Don't worry. You don't have dementia. This is a time of forgetfulness. It is a time of being lost. It, too, will pass.

It is not unusual for people to "act out" at this time. Negative coping strategies are always an option. These are temporary distractions, but they do reduce emotional pain for a short time. Avoidance, which was discussed earlier, is almost always at the heart of these strategies. So affairs, over-drinking, over-eating, over-working, over-sleeping, over-medicating, or relief through pornography are temptations to watch out for. Avoidance tactics can help for a while, like taking an Advil for a headache, but they aren't cures. These tactics always result in more problems and a delayed resolution of grief.

While not addressing each symptom in detail, I would like to focus on one of my most difficult emotional challenges during the grief process—panic attacks. These are a particularly stressful symptom and are prevalent among grieving people. If you have never had one, be grateful.

My first panic attack took me by surprise and was extremely frightening. It happened a week after Austin's death, when friends asked Gary and me out to dinner. We drove by their house to pick them up, and Gary left me in the car while he went inside to get them. A surge of overwhelming panic surfaced instantaneously, causing me to feel disassociated and detached from myself. It was as if there was no anchor to hold on to. The universe had lost its cohesion and boundaries. My panic attack lasted a half-hour, with Gary doing his best to calm me. Somehow, I made it through the night.

That was my first panic attack, but certainly not the last. A few months later, when driving to Houston by myself, I was caught in a traffic jam on the interstate. Flanked by two eighteen-wheelers, it felt like the huge metal vehicles were closing in on me. Suddenly, I thought I was having a heart attack. Crying, sweating, shaking, and gasping for air, I was certain death was moments away.

While grief is not an anxiety disorder, it can lead to one. Some people do need medication to stop the cycle. I started carrying anti-anxiety medication with me and began taking anti-depressants in the second year of my grief process.

About five years later, Gary and I visited a new Sunday school class. We were a little late and came in through the wrong door at the front of the class. It was a large class, with maybe one hundred people all seated and looking at us in surprise. The teacher greeted us and invited us to sit on the front row, quickly resuming his teaching. Suddenly I could not breathe. I jumped up and fled out of the class. My blood pressure had shot up sky-high. It took a minute, but I was finally able to take in air. I learned afterward that I needed to exhale as well as inhale during an attack.

The trigger could have been all the eyes on me or perhaps memories of the funeral, sitting on the front row with people behind me. Often it isn't clear what triggers panic attacks—they seem to come out of nowhere.

One night soon after our oldest son's death, my heart started beating fast. My body shook, and I couldn't breathe. A sense of impending doom overwhelmed me. Gary rushed me to the hospital, only to find that it was another panic attack.

There are ways to manage the attacks. The first step is to recognize it for what it is. Tell yourself, "I'm not dying. I'm having a panic attack, and it will pass." Deep breathing can reduce the fear, but hyperventilating—another symptom—can make things worse. Focus on the breathing: inhale deeply and hold the air in; then exhale deeply.

Close your eyes, relaxing as you breathe in and out. Put yourself in a safe place in your mind. I would picture myself sitting in a swing in a beautiful spot with a long view. I would imagine myself holding and petting my dog. Repeat this process slowly, over and over.

If you are experiencing detachment, focus on something real—the texture of your pants, a glass of cold water, the softness of the grass. This will help to ground you in reality.

You might also try meditation, which helps to remove chaotic thoughts from your mind and replace them with a sense of calm. Meditation is known for relieving stress and anxiety.

Denial and avoidance are normally experienced at the beginning of the grief cycle, although I regressed into denial about four years after our oldest, Wes, died. We were living in the Texas Hill Country, and I decided to pretend Wes was alive, remarried, and living in north Texas. He was happy and fulfilled. In my imagination, I scripted an entirely new life for him. Was I crazy? Perhaps. Was I spending too much time alone? Definitely. I regressed to an earlier stage in my grief, falling back into denial.

Each person travels through their own unique grief stages. Recognizing stages that surface in your own life can help you address them.

When the time is right, read lots of books on grief. It is comforting to see the experiences of others as we all grasp for a lifeline to pull us back to some sort of normalcy. Although we all travel through the same darkness in this journey of grief, we all walk different paths. Our experiences will be different. Some stages will be worse for me, some worse for you. There is a reason it is called "grief work"—none of this is easy.

While the stages of grief are painful to go through, remember that they are to be expected. Something dramatic and unbelievable has happened. We should honor our tremendous loss of a child with a giant pause in our lives. We feel as though everything should stop. And it should. It is right to grieve—but always with the hope and expectation that the deep sorrow will eventually subside, and we will all emerge from the shadows into the light.

Prayer for Today

Lord, this is agony. I'm a mess of wounded and broken places. I'm consumed with the pain with no room for anything else. Help me! Lead me! Spirit, help me in my weakness. I do not even know how I ought to pray. Intercede for me through wordless groans as You promised. Amen.

CHAPTER SEVEN

The Weight of Words: Hearing the Good, the Bad, and the Necessary

"Now when Job's three friends heard of all this
adversity that had come upon him, they came each
one from his own place... Then they sat down
on the ground with him for seven days and seven
nights with no one speaking a word to him, for they
saw that his pain was very great."

—Job 2:11, 13

SONG TO HEAL YOUR HEART

"Be OK" by Ingrid Michaelson

People often ask me, "What should I say to someone who has lost a child?" The truth is, there are no right words.

The passage quoted above comes after Job lost all his possessions and all of his children. The essential words for us are these:

"[His friends] sat down on the ground with him for seven days and seven nights with no one speaking a word to him."

That is excellent advice: *They sat with him, with no one speaking a word.*

For grieving people, there are no right words. What matters is presence. Looking back on my journey through grief, what I remember most, what meant the most, were the people who came to be with me, often in silence.

Author Joe Bayly suffered the death of three of his seven children at early ages. In his book *The View from a Hearse*, he tells of an exchange with two people.

> I was sitting, torn by grief. Someone came and talked to me of God's dealings, of why it happened, of hope beyond the grave. He talked constantly, he said things I knew were true.
>
> I was unmoved, except to wish he'd go away. He finally did.
>
> Another came and sat beside me. He didn't talk. He didn't ask leading questions. He just sat beside me for an hour or more, listened when I said something, answered briefly, prayed simply, left.
>
> I was moved. I was comforted. I hated to see him go.[7]

Although there are no right words for those who are grieving, there are many words that can hurt. Certainly, that is unintended. I decided early on not to hold on to offenses. It is important to remember that people mean well and wish to help.

A Portrait of Grief

As grievers, we are not interested in platitudes and trite assurances. Don't be shocked to hear, "He's in a better place." Or, "She's in heaven with the Lord." Although that may be true, we don't want to hear it. We want our children beside us. Now! We don't want to hear assurances that we will be better soon. It is true that we probably will be, but we don't want to hear it.

We don't want to hear someone say, "I know how you feel," unless they also have suffered the same extreme loss. We don't want to hear, "Your child is now with you all the time, an angel on your shoulder." What we want is our living, breathing child. No one would trade that for an angel on the shoulder, even if it were true. I was told the angel on the shoulder myth many times, even by those who had lost children. If they need to believe this to get through life, I wouldn't want to take their comfort away. I just don't see any scriptural basis to justify that belief.

Trite assurances can enrage us or confuse us. Don't think you are wrong to be angry but try to remember that people really do want to bring comfort and relieve your pain. In tragic situations like the loss of a child, everyone is lost, and everyone is only trying their best.

Some well-intentioned people will offer Christian theology, hoping to help. Don't feel bad if you aren't ready for theological discussions. There does come a time when we can find encouragement through theology and Scripture, just not in the beginning. Understand that no one can completely enter into what you are experiencing. Don't blame them. Who would really want to? I couldn't when I visited others who had lost their children before I lost my own. I wanted to pay my respects and leave as quickly as possible. I couldn't bear their tragedies nor imagine their pain.

What we need most are people who care enough for us to just be there, to stick by us. The "being there" is not a cure, but it does bring comfort and solace. It is the best others can do. To suffer with someone doesn't mean to fully identify with their grief. Don't expect that. I doubt that is even possible, for suffering is, for the most part, a solitary experience. To suffer with another means to be there in whatever way you can, being sensitive to their needs. We don't need others telling us how we should act or react.

Gentle and gracious people are the best comforters to have around you.

There is no cure. There is no fixing this. Don't look to others for a cure. The best others can do is to offer their companionship. What we mourners need most, in the beginning, are listeners. In the first weeks after a tragic loss, there is a great need to tell the story again and again. When I found myself repeating the story to the same neighbor after our grandson's death, I felt embarrassed. I could sense her resistance to hearing, yet again, what must have seemed to be my rantings. I stopped in the middle of the story and changed the subject. If that happens to you, don't be embarrassed. Just choose your confidants wisely. It quickly becomes clear who they are. There is often a strange kind of celebrity that accompanies tragedy. You become a center of interest to others. Be careful of sharing confidences with those you don't know and trust.

Don't be shocked if you are told, "Just get over it." Or, "Isn't it time to move on?" I heard phrases like this more times than I care to count.

Three years after losing our youngest son, our pastor said to me, "Get over it, Cheryl! It has been *three years!* You have three other children who are living. Enjoy them. If you are still grieving after this length of time, you must be caught up in some sin, for you aren't receiving the grace of God."

Angry, I responded, "Pastor, not even God can forget the one who is lost!"

My pastor wasn't trying to be mean, although the words deeply hurt at the time. But he was certainly wrong. We never forget our children!

Several years after that conversation, while on a ladies group trip to Paris, an older woman sat down beside me. She patted my arm and said, "I've never had a chance to tell you how sorry I was about your son. You know, we lost a child. She only lived for four days." And she started to cry. Her daughter had died sixty years earlier.

As George R. R. Martin says in *A Game of Thrones*, "Some old wounds never truly heal and bleed again at the slightest word."

Not only is it unhelpful to hear suggestions that we should "get over" our grief, but it is also hurtful. We are extra sensitive, and insensitive words hurt. When in grief, we often feel guilty. To suggest that we are becoming a bore with a cloud of sadness around us causes more guilt. We already feel crazy. Suggesting that we are going on in unnatural ways increases that sense of craziness and causes us to withdraw at a time when our greatest need is connection.

One of the most difficult moments is when, after losing your child, you are asked for the first time, "How many children do you have?"

For us, it occurred a month after Austin's death. We were photographing a golf course at Horseshoe Bay for the developer. We were invited to have dinner in the home of the club manager with several other couples that lived in their neighborhood. During dinner, our hostess asked me *the* question: "Tell me about your children. How many did you say you have?" I froze. The words would not come, and I could not respond. For the first time, I was called upon to acknowledge with my own voice that our youngest son was dead. And I couldn't.

It was awkward for everyone as the silence grew. My husband jumped in and explained the situation, much to everyone's horror.

There is no helping how others will react to the news of tragedy, but we can be prepared for how we will react to such situations. Choose your words early. Try to decide now what you want to say to others when the dreaded question arises.

I always include my deceased children and say we have four. If a new acquaintance presses for ages or what are they doing now or where they live, I am able now to give more details. I say we have a son in Beaumont, a daughter in College Station, and two of our sons are deceased. If they ask what happened, as they often do, I say, 'I'd rather not talk about it," which is most often the truth. As time goes on and the acquaintance deepens, I may share details, but that is my choice. We don't owe others an explanation of our sorrows. Often in the past, I would rush on to say that we have eight grandchildren in order to leave the conversation on a positive note. Now that we have also lost our dear, oldest grandson, I don't make that comment anymore. It is just too overwhelming for others.

Most parents I have talked with include their lost children in the answer to this question. Most just say, "We have two children," even if they have lost one. When someone presses further about ages or place of residence, they may acknowledge that one lives in heaven or that one is deceased. Most choose not to discuss the cause of the death. Time and practice will make this all easier.

A Portrait of Grief

When suicide was the cause of death, one must think hard about how to handle the question. It does carry a stigma and is a more uncomfortable situation for everyone.

I have always chosen to be honest. Many suicide survivors decide to alter the details to be less shocking. I've never chosen that option. That being said, I really hate the word *suicide*, so I don't say it. Most often, if I decide to give an answer, I will say, "Our oldest son died of depression." No one has ever asked a question after that statement. Sometimes my husband will say, "He died by his own hand." Or "He took his own life." No one asks a question after those statements either.

Perhaps it is easier on others to just say, "It's hard to discuss." Or "Let's not talk about that now."

Although we are free to decide how we will respond to others' questions, I don't think it is best to attempt to keep suicide a secret. Secrets can be deadly within a family. Families who have suffered a suicide don't owe the world anything. Think and pray this through, preparing for this dreaded question.

Some questions seem natural and innocent, such as "How are you?" This is such a common greeting that it doesn't seem like it would cause a problem, but it often does. I have even heard myself ask the same thing of grievers, and I should know better. As a grieving parent, it is difficult to answer since we usually don't know how we are. Therefore, the answer depends upon the relationship with the one asking. With a close friend, I might be totally honest and admit my devastation. With acquaintances, I would just say something like, "I'm okay," or "We are managing," or "It's a hard time right now."

Experts say that the healthiest families are the ones that encourage the expression of their emotions out loud, in words.

As we recognize and communicate our feelings, we move toward resolution and life.

After our youngest son's death, we had some older friends ask us over for dinner. They had lost their youngest son, David, years before. He was hit by a car in front of their home while riding his bike across the street. A neighbor's pile of limbs blocked the driver's view of the boy.

David's father, Bill, told the story. "I removed all pictures of David and all family pictures that included him from the walls and the tabletops in our home. I forbade Joan and our three children from speaking David's name again. That was a terrible mistake! We all grieved alone. Everyone's grief was forced underground."

The result was complicated grief and the delay of their healing. Bill encouraged us to speak of our son often and to keep his pictures out to remember him at his lively best.

Grief won't be denied. In denying grief, we risk a hardening of our hearts. We run the danger of losing our ability to experience and hear the life-giving voice and presence of our God.

While we avoid many conversations that we aren't ready to engage in, and while we shut down conversations that pry at the wrong time, we must not engage in a cover-up. We must allow the intense feelings a way out. Words are our allies in releasing the pressure. While we aren't required to answer others, we really need to find ways to share our pain in order to move forward.

Author Danielle Bernock says, "Trauma is personal. It does not disappear if it is not validated. The silent screams continue internally heard only by the one held captive. When someone enters the pain and hears the screams, healing can begin."[8]

Pain is not to be avoided or denied in this world. The pain we create avoiding pain, however, is avoidable.

If you find yourself in the role of a parent who has lost a child, I pray that many sensitive, compassionate people will come to be with you. If you find yourself in the role of a comforter to one who has lost a child, please don't stay away. Bring your tears and your hugs and your listening ears to the scene of the most devastating losses. You can encourage healing with your presence and care.

Prayer for Today

Father, what does it mean to "get over it"? How do I fill the emptiness within me? Where do I go from here? I have no answers, and yet questions fly at me from all directions. Have mercy, Lord. The only voice I yearn to hear is Yours. Speak to me. Amen.

CHAPTER EIGHT

The Giant of Fear: Being Afraid Is Natural, But It Need Not Last Forever

"The Lord is my light and my salvation;
Whom should I fear?
The Lord is the defense of my life;
Whom should I dread?"

— Psalm 27:1

SONG TO HEAL YOUR HEART

"Whom Shall I Fear?" by Chris Tomlin

Growing up, I was terribly afraid of the dark.

My brother and I shared a bedroom and bed, at least until he started middle school when my daddy finished out the attic to make him an upstairs bedroom.

We didn't have a chest for our clothes in our bedroom, so they were kept in my parents' bedroom. With no overhead light, their room was always dark. I would have to run into their dark room to retrieve my pajamas from the bottom drawer of their dresser every night. Countless times I jammed my fingers, rushing to get them quickly out of the heavy drawer.

Even on the hottest of Texas nights with no air-conditioner and only an attic fan for survival, I loaded the covers over myself for protection. And I *had* to touch my brother to reassure myself he was there. He would have none of it. Every night we would go through the "don't touch me" ritual. I would reach a finger or toe over to touch him for safety, hoping he wouldn't notice. "Don't touch me!" rang out over and over in our room throughout our childhood. Sometimes I accomplished my goal, waiting until he fell asleep before the touch or settling for a touch on the fabric of his pajama top.

"What are you so afraid of?" my brother would demand.

"I don't know," I would answer.

"Don't be afraid!" he commanded me.

"Okay," I whimpered, my mind filled with images of the alligators hiding beneath my bed.

C. S. Lewis's now-famous words equate grief to the feeling of fear: "No one ever told me that grief felt so like fear. I am not afraid, but the sensation is like being afraid. The same fluttering in the stomach, the same restlessness, the yawning. I keep on swallowing. At other times it feels like being mildly drunk or concussed. There is a sort of invisible blanket between the world and me."[9]

Not only does grief feel like fear, but grief also *creates* fear. But what exactly is it about grief that causes fear? It seems that fear in grief is different from other fears we experience. This fear is both rational and irrational! What we most fear has happened.

A Portrait of Grief

It is not just an unformed specter—the dread of something that *might* happen—drifting along outside of reality. This is real, horribly real. Fear is a giant that lurks around the "valley of the shadow of death."

When the worst has already happened, why does the fear grow, getting bigger and bigger? If I could give the Giant of Fear a middle name, it would be "the unknown." As we stare into the abyss, we can't see God. Fear is like the unseen gator under my bed. The longer I dwelled on him, the larger he got.

Just as the children of Israel were met by spies telling them of the giants that barred them from the Promised Land, we are bombarded from within and without by fearful images, doubts, and lies.

Paul David Tripp says fear is spiritual warfare because "our hearts are always a battleground between fear and faith, between doubt and hope, and between what is true and what is false."[10]

Grief intensifies the fear, the doubt, and the false. While we do have spiritual resources to overcome, we seem powerless to lay hold of them. In our paralysis, we are assaulted by fear of our children's suffering, doubt in God's goodness, unable to bear the truth. Life has lost its certainty. Life is now filled with the unknown and full of questions:

- Will we survive this?
- Where is my loved one?
- Is God real?
- Is this a punishment?
- What happens next?

Some fear brought on by grief is irrational. I asked our son Monty whether fear had affected his life after losing his brothers.

"Yes," he said. "I have irrational fears. I used to make fun of people who were afraid of elevators, snakes, heights, or driving. Now I'm one of them. I have a lot of those fears. Something happened in my head when my second brother died. The fear is painful to live with. I don't scoff anymore at people with mental health issues. I have a lot more sorrow and a lot more sympathy."

Monty did the hard things when Wes died. He was the one who went to Houston to pick up Wes's three kids and, with his wife, Holly, kept them for days. He took care of many details and repairs. He spared us all that he could but has paid a high price.

My husband—accustomed to climbing high towers, hanging out of airplanes, and striding on narrow bridges while making photographs—found himself frozen by fear on the Rainbow Bridge. The Rainbow Bridge is the tallest bridge in Texas, spanning the Neches River, with an eighteen-inch walkway across it. He had worked on that high, narrow, and car-jammed bridge many times, but after Wes's death found himself unable to move for fear.

The fear factor can cross over into anxiety and PTSD. It's hard sometimes to distinguish between where one starts and where it ends.

Grief distorts our vision. I have a friend who lost one of her daughters in a four-wheeler accident. When she heard the news, she shut her eyes tight and refused to open them. It was several days before she was coaxed into opening her eyes.

We cannot shut out death by simply shutting our eyes. But we can shut out the light, and fear is always magnified by darkness.

Just as scary television shows are scarier at night, the weight of grief is heaviest in the darkness. When a real nightmare impacts our lives, the world can assume an ongoing darkness. We feel lost and vulnerable, afraid of the most common experiences. Even driving a car can bring unbearable terror.

Most of all, after losing our loved ones, we need light. We need something to look toward. Hope is the distant twinkle that keeps us going. Only the Lord offers us hope. There is nowhere else to turn.

Hope is a special gift given by God through His grace to combat the most difficult circumstances. When despair makes us unable to see any hope for the future, the words of Scripture encourage us to look beyond the immediate heartache. Fear makes us forgetful. But we must remember! Our children are with the Lord, who is faithful and still in control. Even though our emotions are out of control, we are not as powerless as we feel. Read Scripture and be reminded of all that you know to be true.

Fear is also heightened when we are alone. Don't isolate yourself for too long. I know it is tempting to do so, but it isn't healthy. I am an introvert and have always needed alone time. I could have gone into my room and stayed there. But my life would not allow that. Those who loved me wouldn't allow that. I had my daughter calling daily to pull me out of bed with her words. We all need someone to come close and stay beside us in the dark and frightening times of life. We need the corner of someone's pajama top to grasp.

Our God promises to be that one: "For I am the Lord your God who takes hold of your right hand and says to you, Do not fear; I will help you" (Isaiah 41:13, NIV).

And the Apostle Paul tells us, "For God has not given us a spirit of timidity, but of power and love and discipline" (2 Timothy 1:7). The spirit of fear does not belong in believers. It is not given by our God.

Amid grief, we have no human weapons to help us. We must pick up the armor of God. The description of spiritual armor in Ephesians 6 includes an invisible shield of faith for protection against the doubt and despair that assaults us. We must take hold of the "sword of the Spirit," which is the Word of God, full of His promises.

Jesus came to cast out all of our fears. He constantly said, "Don't be afraid." Now more than ever, I must take Him at His word. I must discipline my imagination and my thoughts to believe His words to me:

- "Have I not commanded you? Be strong and courageous! Do not be terrified nor dismayed, for the Lord your God is with you wherever you go" (Joshua 1:9).
- "Peace I leave with you, My peace I give to you; not as the world gives do I give to you. Do not let your heart be troubled nor let it be fearful" (John 14:27).
- "I sought the Lord, and He answered me; and delivered me from all my fears" (Psalm 34:4).
- "Even though I walk through the valley of the shadow of death, I fear no evil, for You are with me; Your rod and Your staff, they comfort me" (Psalm 23:4).

A Portrait of Grief

- "And the peace of God, which surpasses all comprehension, will guard your hearts and your minds in Christ Jesus" (Philippians 4:7).

At the time that our youngest son died, I was leading a women's study group that met in a large home. We had five book studies going on in that home aimed toward reaching unchurched women in our community. We would gather in the spacious living room, sing a song, and I would give a short devotional before breaking into our small groups.

The week after Austin's funeral, I returned to the group for the last time before resigning. I needed time to grieve. After addressing the group about our loss, I opened the floor for prayer requests. It was shocking to hear of so many tragedies, sicknesses, and troubles the women spoke of. I realized that our family had not been singled out for suffering. No one escapes suffering in this world. That's where we live, in the frightening land of suffering. Jesus warned us in his words recorded by John 16:33, "In the world you have tribulation, but take courage; I have overcome the world."

In faith, taking hold of the sword of the Spirit, confronting fear with a shout of undaunted faith, we can conquer the most fearful giant.

Prayer for Today

Lord, I believe! Help my unbelief. Thank you for Your Word. Thank you for Your faithfulness in the past. But, Lord, I can't do this. I want to be strong and courageous, but I am afraid.

Give me faith to trust You even now. You must be strong in me, for I am undone. Send light to flood the day ahead. Speak to me brave words. Be present with and strengthen others who suffer. Direct my thoughts away from the frightening giants surrounding me. Help me to look only at You. In Jesus' name, I pray, Amen.

CHAPTER NINE

Guilt and Grace: Overcoming the Curse of Shoulda, Woulda, and Coulda

"But he was pierced for our transgressions, he was crushed for our iniquities; the punishment that brought us peace was on him, and by his wounds we are healed."

— Isaiah 53:5, NIV

SONG TO HEAL YOUR HEART

"River of Grace" by Christy Nockels

Where there is death, there is guilt. At least that has been my experience. Don't be surprised to find guilt stalking your quiet moments.

Whatever we have done, we could always have done more, been more, and said more to have changed the course of events that ended in the death of our child.

Or could we have?

Chris Martin and his band Coldplay have a song named "The Scientist." In the song, Chris presents himself as a scientist who is so caught up in his work or in figures and progress that he neglects his girlfriend. Chris said this song is based on his "disasters with girls." The video went on to win three MTV awards for its use of the reverse narrative. (You might want to view the official video on YouTube.)

The song and video meant something different to me when I viewed it. Chris declares his desire to go back to the beginning. "Nobody said it would be easy, nobody said it would be so hard," he croons. That starts a rewind on his life. He is seen stepping backward over city sidewalks, railroad tracks, fields, and forests, moping among upward-rising leaves. Backward and backward, he marches—back to the scene of a frightening car crash.

He reseats himself in the wrecked car as the girl we see lying on the ground is miraculously revived and lifted back into the car through a shower of glass. The car continues to reverse back onto the road, past the swerving truck, and on its way backward to a normal and happy life.

If only.

If only that were possible. We are not allowed to live our lives backward, and yet, sadly, that is exactly what grieving parents do. Yearly, daily, hourly, we march ourselves back through our lives, picking out points and envisioning shoulda, woulda, coulda actions that might have changed the outcome.

As comic strip genius Bill Watterson says, "There's no problem so awful that you can't add some guilt to it and make it even worse."

Guilt is a powerful emotion. It can destroy our health, confidence, self-respect, and peace of mind. After losing our youngest son, I felt guilty because I had not grounded him that weekend. He really deserved it for being disrespectful. Knowing we were photographing a wedding and would be out until close to midnight, I held my tongue and skipped the punishment. We had been leaving him alone too much that week already due to work. He had plans with his friends, and I let him go.

My last phone conversation with our oldest son the night before his death left me with massive guilt. It wasn't my words that continued to plague me; it was my silent disapproval of something he said. Later I feared he had sensed my thoughts and my judgment. Did that play a part in his decision to end his life by suicide?

Something else to be aware of is "false guilt." Much of the guilt I experienced, blaming myself for our boys' deaths, was probably unjustified and unwarranted. It often occurs in the grief process. We feel guilty but didn't do anything wrong. Grief is famous for laying all responsibility upon our shoulders even when we are innocent. Examine the truth of your guilty feelings carefully. Are you suffering simply because we live in a fallen world? We aren't responsible for everything that happens.

Guilt and regret drag us back into a dark place in our minds that we can't escape easily. We regret the things we said or didn't say. We regret the things we did or didn't do. We regret the things we coulda, shoulda, woulda done had we been better informed.

The truth is, we are not omniscient. Most of us do the best we can with the information we have at the time. It doesn't really help to know that, does it? We keep attempting a do-over. When we can't go back, and when we can't make amends, what do we do? How do we break the cycle?

We can ask for forgiveness.

Guilt should drive us to repentance. As the Apostle Paul tells us: "Yet now I am happy, not because you were made sorry, but because your sorrow led you to repentance. For you became sorrowful as God intended and so were not harmed in any way by us. Godly sorrow brings repentance that leads to salvation and leaves no regret, but worldly sorrow brings death" (2 Corinthians 7:9–10, NIV).

I suffered over my regrets and failings for years, finally experiencing a step toward healing during a trip to the Holy Land. My husband and I traveled to Israel with Links Players golf ministry. During the trip, I found myself alone with Jeff Cranford, the president of Links Fellowship and the leader of the trip. We were both claustrophobic and did not enter the underground walkway in Jerusalem.

As we walked above ground to meet the group that was walking through the tunnel beneath the old city, Jeff began to share some difficulties he had encountered in his life. Sometime during our conversation, I spoke of my guilt over my boys, my failings, and my remorse. After listening, he said, "In a little while, we will be going to the King's Praetorium, where Jesus was scourged, insulted, spit upon, and crowned with thorns before being led to his death. I think you will see that it was enough."

"What do you mean?" I asked.

"Whatever you did or didn't do, you will see that Jesus paid the price for your mistakes. He took the beating for you, and it was brutal. You don't need to keep beating yourself."

As I began to meditate on the great price Jesus paid for my forgiveness, I read Revelations 12:10, and the words of the Apostle John spoke to me: "Then I heard a loud voice saying in heaven, 'Now the salvation, and the power, and the kingdom of our God and the authority of His Christ have come, for the accuser of our brothers and sisters has been thrown down, the one who accuses them before our God day and night.'"

I could see clearly that my guilt was the result of accusations by Satan, the enemy of my soul. When I agreed with him, joining my voice to his as he accused me, and continued to wallow in my guilt and regret, I had crossed a line. I had joined Satan in discounting the suffering of Jesus. Jeff had been right—it was enough.

I began to talk back to my guilt. Each time it would move to the front of my mind, I would remind myself of the suffering Jesus endured to purchase my forgiveness. Asking our Lord for forgiveness acknowledges that we were wrong. We did something wrong, spoke something wrong, or thought something wrong. Asking our God for forgiveness and acknowledging that He was broken *for* us brings restoration. Grace is heaped upon our heads, and mercy is poured over our feet as the Lord washes us clean with His own forgiveness.

Isn't it time for you to move forward, too? There should be no guilty Christians.

We yearn to be better mothers, fathers, daughters, sons, grandkids, brothers, sisters, and friends. We can be that, but only as we move forward and leave guilt behind.

Prayer for Today

Lord, thank you for all that You suffered to spare me suffering. Forgive me for any hurt I have caused. Please bring them to my mind, one by one, that I might acknowledge my sins before You. Forgive me. Please, oh Lord, assure my heart of Your forgiveness and silence the enemy's voice. Strengthen me to move forward to be the person You see in me. I ask in the name of Jesus, who purchased my forgiveness and Your grace at such a high cost. Amen.

CHAPTER TEN

Learning to Receive Comfort: I Know How You Feel

"Blessed be the God and Father of our Lord
Jesus Christ, the Father of mercies and God of all
comfort, who comforts us in all in our affliction so
that we will be able to comfort those who are in any
affliction with the comfort with which we ourselves
are comforted by God."

— 2 Corinthians 1:3–4

SONG TO HEAL YOUR HEART

"Angels Among Us" by Alabama

As the primary caregiver to my mother for many years, a helper for my dad in the last year of his life, and the mother of four children, I learned how to give comfort. I just never learned how to receive it.

With our parents always preoccupied with one another and their relationship, my brother and I learned to go it alone emotionally. We tended to our own wounds. When one of us skinned a knee or got a cut, my mother would have to lie down. We would get her a wet cloth and place it over her face to keep her from fainting.

As my brother tells it: "Mother, bless her, would faint at the sight of blood. When I was young, I had many, many scrapes and cuts that drew blood. I would run home, open the back door, and call for Mother to come to the door. Without even glancing at my injury, she would hand me appropriate materials for me to treat myself—towel, rubbing alcohol, mercurochrome, Band-Aids, gauze, whatever was needed to clean and secure the injury. There was never a thought of stitches—we had duct tape! Neither was there ever a thought of seeing a doctor."

Although I never learned to receive comfort as a child, God did send His people to comfort me in my times of greatest need.

After Austin's death, our huge rural mailbox was stuffed with notes and cards for an entire year. Every day for a year! One person who remains anonymous sent an encouraging note each day throughout the year. When, at the end of the year, I came home to find only the normal mail, I left a note and a gift in the mailbox for the postal carrier, thanking her for carefully handling all our mail. She left a note of thanks and said, "It has been an amazing outpouring of love."

One morning in the second year of my grief, I had four friends appear at our door. We still lived out in the country, so the drop-in guests were quite unexpected. Although it was ten o'clock, I was still in my nightgown and in bed. Peeping through the door and recognizing my friends from church, I let them in. They had come to sing to me, which they did as I sat on the green couch, absorbing their love and God's love and comfort for me.

When each of our boys died, people came to the house and stayed with us. They brought food and drinks, cooked meals, served us, and cleaned up. They gave us fresh sheets, placed flowers through the house, and put roses on my pillow. Our front porch was filled with potted plants brought by thoughtful people. Friends gave money to memorial funds and offered their beach houses and lake houses for our respite care. They offered to take us on trips and gave us tickets to concerts. They brought musical recordings to us at our studio and their special dishes like cakes, pies, or stuffed artichokes (my favorite).

One area restaurant sent us gift certificates to come and eat that were underwritten by the staff. The cleaners wouldn't take payment for rush cleaning the dress I wore to the funeral. My hairdresser came to my house to do my hair. A realtor we had never met paid a caterer to have casseroles sent to the house for a period of time in the weeks following Wes's funeral. The outpouring of love and compassion was astonishing.

Comfort touched us and opened us and ministered to us. Again and again, as we moved from community to community and experienced loss after loss, the people of Christ extended their healing hands and blessed us with their grace.

We experienced what Richard Attenborough, in his narration of the film *Mother Theresa*, calls a light in this world, which he describes as "A healing spirit more powerful than any darkness we may encounter. We sometimes lose sight of this force when there is suffering and too much pain. Then suddenly the Spirit will emerge through the lives of ordinary people who hear the call and answer in extraordinary ways."[11]

By now, I have been in the homes of many people visited by tragic and traumatic death. I know my experience is not everyone's experience. I know that many, many people do not receive the tremendous outpouring of support that came our way. If that is your story, I can only say, "I'm sorry." I wish it were different for you. Just remember that you are not alone in your grief. If you have surrendered your life to the God of all comfort, then He is there with you, and that will be enough. If you have never asked the living Lord to enter your heart and accepted His offer of new life and peace, then now is a good time to do that.

I'm sure much of the loving attention we received was due to our work, which put us in the public eye. Also, our children were involved in many activities and had a wide array of acquaintances. We were active members of a large church. There have been many times in my life when I have looked out of my window and wished for God to send one of His people down my front walk to comfort me—and no one came. Why God allowed the deaths of our children to break the hearts of so many is a mystery. I can only say that the loving concern poured out on us was a comfort only our Lord could have orchestrated.

Loss and hard transitions bind us to people in unexpected ways. I'm reminded of this when I recall the time one of our sons wrecked his car in college. Gary said we couldn't afford to buy him another at that time. Our son went for a while without a car, which created difficulties. He couldn't keep his job, and he couldn't come home from school.

I had a new Ford LTD, which I decided to trade in for two used cars—one for him and an ugly but reliable Aerostar van for me.

I had never noticed an Aerostar van before, but suddenly I saw them everywhere. The parking lots were full of them. I passed them on highways and saw them parked at friends' houses. Now I was one of them—an Aerostar van owner.

It's that way with people who have lost children. Once you become "one of them," they appear from out of nowhere. Untold people wrote, called, and came to share their own stories. I found the only people I really wanted to see were the ones who were "one of us."

They are the only ones who could say, "I know how you feel."

In 1984, humanitarian activist Jerry White lost his leg in a landmine accident while hiking with friends through northern Israel. This loss dictated the direction of his life for many years as he recovered and then learned to live life despite the horror on the minefield. In 1996, Jerry took a trip to Cambodia, where he saw countless amputees. Millions of landmines were left behind after decades of conflict.

Jerry had an experience that changed his life. "As I walked along the streets of Phnom Penh," he said, "a little girl hopped up to me. She couldn't have been more than eight or nine years old, clearly not a combatant in the wars of Cambodia. She smiled broadly at me, pointed at my $17,000 prosthetic leg, and said, 'You are one of us.' She leaned on her homemade crutch, and I realized she was right."[12]

That chance meeting and that little girl's words spurred Jerry to examine what he could do to help the hundreds of thousands of disabled people like her. He started the Landmine Survivors' Network, setting out to ban the use of landmines and helping survivors get prosthetic legs and find work.

We long to know that others understand our pain and can truly empathize with our experiences. After losing our youngest son, the Lord spoke to my heart, "Don't push me away, Cheryl. I know how it feels to lose a son."

There is a modern-day parable that I've heard from different pulpits over the years. It features a father who worked as a switchman for a railroad. One day he takes his young son with him to work. It is the switchman's job to control the movement of the tracks using levers that must be switched for the train to safely avoid another traveling train or to safely cross a bridge. On this particular day, as the train was approaching, the man sees his young son playing in the gears of the track. The man is faced with an impossible choice: flip the switch to secure the correct position of the tracks, thereby crushing his son, or allow the passenger train to run off the track into the abyss, saving his son.

After a moment's hesitation, shutting his eyes, he flips the switch and watches the passengers through the train windows laugh, sip their tea, and read their books, oblivious of the great sacrifice he has made in sacrificing his son. This is a picture of God's love. He sacrificed His own son to save us. He is indeed "one of us."

After each of our boys died, I thought of that story, knowing I would never have made that choice. I would have allowed every car on Highway 105 to endure a fatal crash if it had saved my son. I would have traded ten trainloads of strangers for any one of our boys.

Yes, our God is "one of us." He knows the agony, the pain of losing a child. He understands our pain. I am the one who struggles to understand the Lord. How could He watch as His son was crushed for you and for me?

I want to scold God, telling Him even if His son needed to die for others to be saved and have life, mine didn't! But while I know the truth that only Christ's life and death can save, I also know that many others chose life in Christ due to our losses.

A Portrait of Grief

When you are with someone who has been there before you, when you feel cared for and understood, know that God has also been with you, for He is the source of all comfort.

Prayer for Today

Oh, Lord, Your love is incomprehensible. I surrender my suffering to You. Use the hard things of my life to produce good in the lives of others. Comfort me so that I can learn to comfort others. Grant me mercy so I can learn to be merciful. I know You never leave me alone in my suffering. Teach me to stick wholeheartedly with others in their suffering. Thank you for the angels among us. Bless them mightily, dear Lord. I ask this in the name of Jesus, who gave Himself up for us. Amen.

CHAPTER ELEVEN

Special Days: When They're Not So Special Anymore

"Can a woman forget her nursing child And have no compassion on the son of her womb? Even these may forget, but I will not forget you."

— Isaiah 49:15

SONG TO HEAL YOUR HEART

"Goodbye" by Kenny Rogers

When you have lost someone dear to you, holidays, birthdays, and other special days throughout the year take on an entirely different meaning. They usually become painful rather than joyful. They bring up memories that cause you to smile but also to cry. They prompt you to remember wonderful times of the past while you struggle to step toward the future.

Birthdays and Anniversaries

The summer is over—the trees know, the birds know, the children know. Fall marks the day. The end of life as it should be.

I'll not look at a calendar for September, I tell myself, *then I won't know when the day I lost my child comes or when it goes.*

Who was I kidding? As the earth knows of summer's end, as the sun knows when to yield to the night—so a mother's heart knows the day her child died. Fathers and siblings feel the oppression as well. We all share the drama of losses that will always remain a part of our life stories. Yes, birthdays and death days won't be ignored, and they are always hard.

Although I usually try not to look at the calendar in those months, my body always tells me. Austin died in September, and I start to feel the sadness when there is the smell of fall in the air, along with the sight of a yellow school bus reminding me that it is time to start school.

Pollen and spring flowers cause my heart to break, for Wes died in the spring, as did his son, our grandson, Brock. Time does help, and the sorrow lessens as years go by. But the pain is always there, like a sad song playing in the background of our happy times, growing softer and softer with the passing years.

All family get-togethers will be different, with an empty chair always serving as a reminder. Routine days are easier to manage than times of celebration. How can we celebrate when there is always one too few?

Special days are occasions to give yourself special care and attention. Pace yourself. Remember, healing is a marathon, not a sprint. Don't get too busy. What is it they tell alcoholics? H-A-L-T. Don't get too *hungry, angry, lonely,* or *tired.* That is good advice for someone in grief.

Grievers look for ways to include and remember. That's a good thing. One woman I spoke with said she always includes their deceased child in everything they do. At the time we talked, her family had just returned from a trip to the beach—all fourteen members. That count included her missing son. There is always an empty chair at the table for him at holidays and family dinners.

"We celebrate his birthday at the beach each year," she said.

Our son Monty wrote "happy birthday" poems for Austin on his birthday. He stopped that after losing his older brother Wes. It was just too much—too many brothers gone.

My grief attacks always come a few days before or after the "special" days. Usually, I am surprised that the actual "day" is easier than I anticipated. But that's me. I don't know how it will be for you. There are no rules of observance, but we can and must make our own rules.

I discovered a Jewish tradition that is helpful. This observance begins on the anniversary of the day of death with a candle being lit at sunset. It is called a Yahrzeit candle and is designed to burn for twenty-four hours. Once lit, these candles should be left to burn until they extinguish on their own. I adapted a modified version of this observance. We light a candle on loved ones' death days and on their birthdays. We light them in the morning and let them burn until they burn out or until we go to bed. We read the following prayer in unison:

May God the Father, who remains faithful in life
and death, God's Son, our Lord and Savior Jesus

Christ, whose own death and resurrection give us
the promise of new life, and the power of the Holy
Spirit, whose daily presence transforms our world,
empower our journey towards sanctity and fill us
with the hope of resurrection and new life. Amen.[13]

It is a small ceremony, a small act of remembrance, but it
gives me comfort.

Some people bring out scrapbooks and look at pictures,
talking about their deceased children. We do that, but it is
usually spontaneous—when we are moving or organizing. And
sometimes for no particular reason.

To me, purposeful acts of remembrance are a way to take
control of these difficult milestones.

Thanksgiving

I don't know the sequence in which holidays will arrive in your
life. Thanksgiving and Easter have always been my favorite
holidays and still are. While the chairs are empty and our hearts
are broken, we can give thanks for our blessings at Thanksgiving. It tends to be focused on family and food but also pulls us
toward good memories.

I noticed something during my deepest anguish: When I
praised God and thanked Him for our many blessings, my pain
would subside—not for long, but for a while. Perhaps that is why
we are admonished in Scripture to "in everything give thanks;
for this is God's will for you in Christ Jesus" (1 Thessalonians
5:18).

Christmas

For the first Christmas after losing our youngest child, we stayed at home, having no energy to give it much thought and no inclination to celebrate. Still, Gary insisted on putting up the tree. I cried and cried through the whole process. The little ornaments that our Austin had made in school growing up did me in. We had many friends drop by to visit. Our surviving kids came to Christmas Eve dinner with their spouses. We could scarcely eat because of the many people stopping to give us hugs. Christmas Day was nothing but a blur.

In subsequent years, we all took a trip together somewhere in Texas, staying in a hotel and eating out. After several years, with our three older children married and starting families, we released them to begin spending Christmas with their in-laws or at their own homes. We would celebrate together two weeks before Christmas. We christened it "Christopher Christmas." Gary and I often spent Christmas Eve and Christmas Day together at home or with friends.

I recommend to you not spending the first Christmas alone. Ask someone over or make some special plans if you don't have family around. Do your best to not bring everyone down, but remember you are not Santa Claus, with the need to spread cheer and give gifts. It is not up to you to make everyone happy this year. Be as flexible as you can. Christmas will be different from now on. There will always be someone missing and always an empty spot in your heart.

Being photographers, Gary and I sent family photo cards at Christmas starting the year we married. Our last one was the year our youngest son died. I just couldn't do it without him.

Everyone who has experienced loss handles these traditions differently, so honor yourself and your needs. I have friends who sent cards the year their child died and each year thereafter. One friend who lost a twin always has the surviving twin hold a photo of her sister in their family portraits.

How many Christmas stockings should you hang? I ceased to hang any. I gave them all away. Some people hang stockings for all their children, the ones in town, the two out of town, and the one in heaven. Others hang all but the one of the lost child, placing it on the mantle to signify that the child is missing. Do what feels right to you.

I realize that many of you have young children still living in your homes. Our experience was both easier and harder because we didn't. Early death makes our missing children special, as we tend to remember the good times and dwell on their positive qualities. If you still have children in your home, as best you can, make the living children feel special as well. Try to make the holiday fun for them.

Shopping for gifts can be painful because it is a reminder of purchasing presents for your deceased child. If possible, shop early or online for Christmas. Have someone close to you shop with you for necessary Christmas gifts or ask them to do it for you. My first Christmas, our daughter, Molly, drove me ninety miles away to Houston, and we bought every gift at one store.

Do plan ahead as much as possible. Make meal planning simple. Don't pressure yourself or your family with too many activities. Grief takes an enormous amount of energy. Try to get lots of rest, drink water, and watch your alcohol intake. Alcohol and grief don't mix well.

How do you respond when people say, "Merry Christmas"? Decide ahead of time. It's perfectly acceptable to say a simple "Thank you" or "Merry Christmas to you too."

Throughout the holiday season (and any special days), be especially gentle with yourself and others. If you cry or break down, don't let it ruin the day. Christmas brings powerful memories of our loved ones. It seems that everything—movies, cards, foods, songs—everything is a potential reminder and can trigger grief. Stop, acknowledge, and feel the pain. Share the feelings with someone. Remember, it always helps to get what's on the inside to move to the outside. A good way to do that is by talking about it.

Talk about your child when you want to. Encourage others to talk about them. But try to be sensitive to others and their needs. Our son couldn't and can't talk about his two brothers that he has lost on holidays. We try to respect that when we are with him. Our daughter has no problem talking and listening to me talk about her brothers. We are all different.

Beyond all the carols and the cooking, beyond all the tinsel and the presents, we who have lost our children still have hope. Luke 2:9–11 tells us, "And an angel of the Lord suddenly stood near them, and the glory of the Lord shown around them; and they were terribly frightened. And so the angel said to them, 'Do not be afraid; for behold, I bring you good news of a great joy which shall be for all the people; for today in the city of David there has been born for you a Savior, who is Christ the Lord.'"

We must concentrate our thoughts daily, and especially at Christmas, on the hope that can only come from Christ and the great gift of eternal life offered to us and to our children through His death. Sure, our emotions take us up and down and all around, but the truth of our faith is the rock beneath the heaving and quaking ground.

I like this reminder by Henri Nouwen: "This is the great mystery of Christmas that continues to give us comfort and consolation: we are not alone on our journey. The God of love who gave us life sent us His only Son to be with us at all times and in all places so that we never have to feel lost in our struggles but always can trust that He walks with us."[14]

New Year

After the significant loss of a loved one, how can it possibly be a *happy* New Year? Can it ever be again? As grieving parents, we aren't sure we can face another year of pain and sorrow. We face another 365 days without our children.

We must realize that the intensity of this suffering cannot go on forever. We may not feel that way in the beginning, for, in the beginning, we don't look forward. When we do look forward, the future appears dark and empty. But we know intellectually that it is not true—we will survive. Others who have walked before us testify that it will eventually get easier.

New Year's parties are optional. The good thing about New Year's is that it doesn't typically center around family. The event usually revolves around friends and fun (and often alcohol). If someone in your close circle invites you to a party and you prefer it to sitting at home crying, then try to summon the energy to go. Perhaps it will be a distraction and perhaps will provide a boost for you. Celebrations are difficult and will be for a long time—but it is worth the effort to push yourself into social settings rather than isolating yourself. Above all, be attuned to your needs and give grace to yourself.

We do need to look at the good things in our lives. It is worth repeating to say: focus on Philippians 4:8, "Finally brothers and sisters, whatever is true, whatever is honorable, whatever is right, whatever is pure, whatever is lovely, whatever is commendable, if there is any excellence and if anything worth of praise, think about these things."

Amid grief, the coming year may not hold much promise for happiness, but you can acknowledge the good and determine to accomplish some good. We can love the good that remains. We can love all that we have left.

Easter

This day can center on bunnies and eggs, or we can look to hope in the Resurrection. In Scripture, we observe Jesus as He walks the earth. We watch as He heals the sick, forgives the wrongdoers, embraces the forsaken, and raises the dead. We see Him die young, a death filled with injustice. And then we watch as He overcomes even death and rises on the third day. And He says, "Remember me" as we take the bread and the wine.

Yes, these are the days to remember that death has been defeated. The empty tomb is our powerful assurance that death does not have the final word. It is not a forever parting that we are asked to endure. We will see our children again.

***

On special days do everything you can to care for yourself, receive care from others, and be assured of the care of your loving heavenly Father.

Prayer for Today

Father, I feel the "special days" staring at me across the pages of my calendar. It feels so wrong for time to go on. Celebration is an outrage to me! All of time is divided now into the before and the after. How do I go on? Fill me with the power of Your Spirit. Give me the strength and power and grace and hope to get through this day. In Jesus' name, Amen.

CHAPTER TWELVE

Small Steps, Big Gains: Self-Care Is Not Optional

"I will refresh the weary and satisfy the faint."

—Jeremiah 31:25, NIV

SONG TO HEAL YOUR HEART

"You're Gonna Be Okay" (Lyric Video)
by Brian and Jenn Johnson

Make Rest a Priority

Finding rest in the midst of grief often seems impossible. This is a time for treating yourself gently. Don't attempt new projects. Don't take on new responsibilities. Recovery consumes all the energy available.

I had trouble sleeping for a long time following my losses. I could fall asleep but then wake around 1 a.m., unable to go back to sleep.

Although many sleep experts recommend getting up and doing something when you wake up in the middle of the night, sometimes just resting in bed or on the couch is helpful. Remember, you are in recovery. An intentional time of rest during the day is also vital. It is important to meditate or find some distraction to calm your emotions. Meditation on God's Word in the morning and the last thing at night is helpful. Meditation for a believer is not an emptying of the mind but rather a filling of the mind and heart by God's Spirit.

We read the "living word" of God because it is still His primary way of communicating to us. We can and do hear God's voice in our heads or hearts, knowing that the living word of God cannot and will not deceive. Read His words and think on them.

Ask the Lord to give you rest. Picture yourself laying your burdens on Him while you rest for a while. Remember His promises: "Take my yoke upon you and learn from me, for I am gentle and humble in heart, and you will find rest for your souls" (Matthew 11:29).

Find a Group of Fellow Grievers

Support groups are readily available in almost every community. These groups give an opportunity for people to pour out their feelings in a place where others truly understand. Be sure to find the right group, the right fit, for your needs.

After losing our youngest son, Gary and I attended a grief group. After attending the group several times, I realized that I felt worse, not better, by the experience. We found ourselves in the role of encourager to others. There was a hopelessness and helplessness there that I could not abide.

That group did help me to realize that even in my anger, my hope was securely fastened to the faithfulness of a loving, trustworthy God. At that time, I was not strong enough to be cast into the role of encourager for others lost in their grief. We decided not to continue attending.

Several years later, I joined a grief group and found it extremely helpful. I was asked to lead the group and led for several years until the death of our oldest son. For the time that I attended, those dear people helped to move me toward healing.

If this is something you are ready for, grief groups can be easily found (check out www.griefshare.com). There are ten such groups in my small Texas town. Most communities have these groups that meet in churches or community centers. These are usually free of charge, though some do ask for a modest fee. If you aren't ready for in-person groups, there are grief support workshops online that might suit you.

Above all, remember that isolating yourself is not healthy and does not promote healing. It is not wise to try to process your deep feelings alone. We need others in good times, and we really need others in the bad times.

Take this advice to heart from author Ken Gire: "There are things in life we must do alone, but walking through the valley of the shadow of death is not one of them. When we mourn the loss of someone we love, it helps to mourn in community with others who feel the pain of our loss."[15]

Journaling

I agree with the words of William Faulkner: "I never know what I think about something until I read what I've written." That's why I have found the practice of journaling so helpful in processing my thoughts and feelings.

The grieving journey is not a constant upward climb that can be navigated on a linear path, moving straight from sorrow to acceptance. There are stages, but they are not conquered in a steady manner. It is one step forward, two steps back, two steps forward, and one step back. It is a confusing and frustrating pathway. Writing, like talking, allows us to see and examine the steps we are attempting to take, slow and wobbly.

In order to process and heal from a devastating loss, we must talk, talk, talk. If we can't do that, we can write, write, write. At times when our lives are in chaos, writing can bring order into the disorder.

I find it amusing to look back at my journals. They are stacked on a shelf inside a closed cabinet in my bedroom. Some of them are full of my life poured out in words. But many of them are half-full or have a page or two or twenty that have been written upon while the rest of the year is blank.

If you decide to journal, don't make a lot of rules for yourself. Rules will turn into roadblocks. You aren't required to write each day. You don't need to fill an entire page. You should not be perfectionistic, creating award-winning poetry or prose. No one is grading your work! Let the journal serve your needs. It is a private haven where you can express your own feelings, not worrying about what others think.

Create a list of thanksgiving. There are still things to be grateful for—the sunrise, a hot meal, a poodle puppy, a home to enjoy even if it feels empty.

Create a list of accomplishments. I got out of bed today. I exercised. I went to work. I cooked a meal. During grief, these are laudable achievements, and you should record them and applaud yourself.

The whole purpose of a journal is to be a friend who listens as you pour out your heart.

Exercise for Your Body and Soul

Grief is not only emotional; it is extremely physical. Exercise is highly therapeutic. Always. Especially during grief.

Some people prefer strenuous exercise, activating endorphins to achieve a "runner's high" and releasing stress. Others prefer more low-key forms, such as walking, yoga, or tai chi. I continued exercising after each of our losses; typically, taking long walks helped. It was helpful to me and will be for you to have an exercise partner for talking while moving.

Group classes can be a positive at this time. Just slip in late if you want to avoid conversation and leave at the end of the class. I enjoyed a sense of community in a class, especially since the focus was not on me.

During grief, most people either lose or gain weight. I lost twenty pounds when we lost our youngest son, and I gained twenty pounds when we lost our oldest son. It took a long time for me to even care about my weight, up or down. Much more important matters filled my heart and mind.

Exercise also helped me to avoid antidepressant medication for a long time and, when the time came for me to go on it, exercise helped me to be free of them.

The Mayo Clinic says regular exercise helps ease depression and anxiety by releasing feel-good endorphins, natural cannabis-like brain chemicals, and other natural chemicals that can enhance your sense of well-being. It is also helpful in taking your mind off worries so you can get away from the cycle of negative thoughts that feed depression and anxiety.

As little as thirty minutes of walking three to five days a week can help. No walking partner? Listen to uplifting podcasts to keep you company or your favorite music to lift you up.

Be Intentional about Physical Intimacy

The topic of sex may seem odd to discuss in a book on grief and loss. But it can't be ignored. It is a normal part of life. And a healthy and healing part of life when approached wisely. But just like eating and sleeping, sexual patterns may change for a while.

Your spouse may need more sex than ever before. That is not abnormal. Grief can intensify the sex drive in many. You may have the same need, or you may have no desire or energy to participate. Try to understand and accommodate one another.

Sexual intimacy does provide comfort and release. It can bring comfort and be a life-giving experience even during such a difficult time. Even if physical intimacy is not a high desire or need, be intentional about making the time and preserving the energy for it as a way to promote your emotional healing.

If there is no desire or no ability to engage sexually during this time, don't worry about it. Your natural inclinations will return eventually. This is a time of extremes. Be gentle with yourself and with your spouse.

A Portrait of Grief

Adopt a Pet

The month after losing Wes, I adopted a dog.

I had seen miniature poodles in California during a bridal Trunk Show for Saks Fifth Avenue, where I was presenting my bridal gowns. It made me happy just to look at those cuddly pooches.

My husband had always been allergic to dogs, but after searching the internet, I learned that poodles are hypoallergenic. They are also smart, obedient, and anxious to please.

We named him King Louis (pronounced Lou-*ee*) as a nod to my working days in France. Louis was my constant companion and continual comforter. It is a wonder that he ever learned to walk because he spent almost all the time in my arms.

There is a reason therapy dogs are allowed in hospitals, nursing homes, and airplanes. They bring comfort. They improve our blood pressure and enhance our brain chemistry. With loving eyes and wagging tales, they assure us that everything will be okay.

Besides all of this, they make us smile. They give us reason to laugh. They change the subject from sorrows to happiness, from death to life. They give us needed love at a time when that's all that matters.

Louis gave me a reason to live. He made me get up in the morning. He forced me to exercise. After losing Louis when he ran after a deer and couldn't be found (sob!), we found another poodle quickly. We named her Antoinette, calling her Annie. She did her magic healing ministry for thirteen years.

Don't like dogs? How about a goat, a hamster, a fish, you get the idea. As author Nick Trout says,

It may be a cat, a bird, a ferret, or a guinea pig, but the chances are high that when someone close to you died, a pet will be there to pick up the slack. Pets devour the loneliness. They give us purpose, responsibility, a reason for getting up in the morning, and a reason to look to the future. They ground us, help us escape the grief, make us laugh, and take full advantage of our weakness by exploiting our furniture, our beds, and our refrigerator. We wouldn't have it any other way. Pets are our seat belts on the emotional roller coaster of life—they can be trusted, they keep us safe, and they sure do smooth out the ride. [16]

Make Some Art

When we moved to Texas Hill Country, my husband had the time to play a lot of golf. After so many years working and caring for parents and children, there was suddenly little for me to do after morning exercise and chores. We entertained, attempting to build a new network of friends, but that still left too much empty time.

I found a drawing class in San Antonio and began to go once a week. After that class, I took a beginning oil painting class and started painting. We have all heard there is healing power in the arts, but I began to experience it in earnest. Focused on shapes and color, my mind seemed unable to focus on any other thing.

According to art therapist Cathy Malchiodi, the creative process brings healing and reparative trauma recovery. There are now studies showing the benefit of art therapy. The creative process is healing. It is also a powerful form of communication. It is not enough to read about healing—sometimes, we need to act it out through our hands. The point is not the finished product but the actual act of art-making that I found so healing. When all passion was dead to me, I found a new one in painting. Somehow, it soothed my soul.

If you don't want to draw or paint, that's okay. Edith Schaeffer defines the term "Hidden Art" as art found in the minor areas of life. There are countless ways to make art, such as learning to play an instrument, sculpting, gardening, flower arrangement, preparing food, writing, or drama. Some people build birdhouses or take up knitting. Find some creative outlet that soothes your soul. It will reduce your stress and enhance your life.

We must get out of ourselves. I constantly ask the Lord for the gift of self-forgetfulness, but we must work with Him. I bought a piano and played it. Playing an instrument can take you out of yourself. If you played in the band or orchestra in school, consider dragging that old flute or tuba or guitar out of the attic. There is a centering that is calming and leaves room for little else in the mind.

What does the Bible say about creativity? The very first verse of Scripture actually describes the first recorded creative act as "God created the heavens and the earth" (Genesis 1:1). Our heavenly Father is creative and made each of His children to be creative as well—which brings light to our dark moments.

Find Healing in Nature

Scripture tells us,

> But ask the animals, and they will teach you, or
> the birds in the sky, and they will tell you; or speak
> to the earth, and it will teach you, or let the fish
> in the sea inform you. Which of all these does not
> know that the hand of the Lord has done this? In
> his hand is the life of every creature and the breath
> of all mankind.
>
> —Job 12:7–10 (NIV)

Simply put, nature calms our anxiety and heals our wounds. For one thing, sunlight helps boost the brain's chemical serotonin. It gives us energy and an increased sense of well-being. Doctors sometimes treat seasonal affective disorder (SAD) and other types of depression with natural or artificial light. Sunshine also provides a boost in Vitamin D.

My husband and I find comfort at the seashore, driving to a Texas beach as often as we can. The sound of the ocean, the sunshine, the clouds, and the walks on the beach do their healing work. The curative properties of water and the beach cannot be fully documented or explained. I only know that they soothe the soul.

Do you live far from the beach and can't afford to go there? Is there a lake or a river where you can sit in the sun and take in the view? Perhaps there is a public park nearby that celebrates

God's creation. Find a place where you can soak in the sun and beauty. It is healing.

Prayer for Today

Oh, creator God, make us more like You. Breathe Your life-giving air into each of us, and infuse us with Your creative nature, with Your creative power. Bring healing deep into our souls. Amen.

CHAPTER THIRTEEN

Signs and Epiphanies: On the Lookout for Everyday Miracles

"So again I ask, does God give you his Spirit and work miracles among you by the works of the law, or by your believing what you heard?"

— Galatians 3:5, NIV

SONG TO HEAL YOUR HEART

"Where I Find God" by Larry Fleet (Official Live Video)

Earlier I spoke of experiencing the Lord's hand on my shoulder, His presence in the room, and the Spirit pointing out a scripture to me shortly before our grandson's death. It took a while before I could tell anyone of the experience. It felt private and sacred, a holy moment between the Lord and me. I treasured it in my heart.

I was certain that the Father had sent His comforting presence and a physical touch to strengthen me, but should I tell others? When I finally told two of my closest friends, I asked them to please not tell anyone else. Would others think I was a few fries short of a Happy Meal?

Before writing about this, I searched my Bible and read the words of Jesus to me: "What I tell you in the darkness, tell in the light; and what you hear whispered in your ear, proclaim upon the housetops" (Matthew 10:27).

Before the time Jesus spoke these words, he had not fully revealed to Israel and the world that he was the Messiah. In fact, he told many people he had healed not to tell anyone about the experience in order to keep that truth from being fully understood until the right time. But now, Jesus told his disciples it was time to start declaring the truth.

When the time comes, Jesus wants us to broadcast our truths far and wide in a public way. He wants us, His people, to declare from the housetops His powerful work among us.

Years before, when our youngest son died, one of my oldest friends encouraged me to ask God for a sign that Austin was okay and with Him in heaven.

"I don't think God answers requests like that," I responded.

"Seems to me He owes you that," she answered.

I did ask the Lord for a sign.

His answer came quickly to my spirit: "My Word is enough for you." I knew it was true. I had been a believer since I was twelve and had read my Bible consistently since then. I attended a Baptist church that taught the Bible in Sunday school. I went through Bible Study Fellowship and had been a teacher myself. The Lord had already told me in His Word that He would never leave me nor forsake me. He had promised life everlasting. I knew Austin had that promise also.

A Portrait of Grief

And yet, before our grandson Brock's death, the Lord touched me—palpably—on the shoulder. He spoke to me in a way I knew was not my imagination or "wish fulfillment." Although I did not know what the future would hold, I had the assurance that the future was in His hands.

I began to ask other mothers who had lost children if God had given them a supernatural event or an unexpected assurance of His love and their child's security.

One mother, Patricia, was encouraged by sightings of red cardinals. In the devastating days after losing her son, Doug, she received a phone call from a friend who was walking by the house where Doug had lived.

"Patricia, have you seen the cardinals?" the friend asked.

"What cardinals?" Patricia responded.

"Patricia, Doug's yard is filled with cardinals—covered with cardinals. There are none in the yards nearby, just in Doug's yard."

In the days, weeks, and months that passed, cardinals appeared to Patricia everywhere. The last time, she sat alone at the beach in a day of terrible suffering. She asked the Lord if a cardinal could appear to her there as an assurance. As unlikely as it sounds, she heard a sound beside her and saw a cardinal caught in a bush. Sobbing, she promised the Lord that she would never ask Him for a sign again. This experience was reassuring and comforting enough.

The cardinal is symbolic of life and restoration. For Patricia, the appearance of this bird was always a perfect picture of hope.

Another woman I met named Janene had a son, a young doctor, who developed a chronic cough. Taylor died just months later of an aggressive and rare form of lung cancer. When I asked her about signs or epiphanies after Taylor's death, she said, "Yes, I have had such experiences. But if I tell you about them, Cheryl, you're going to think I'm crazy. I don't tell many people."

I assured Janene that I certainly would not think she was crazy. I believe God speaks to people and meets people in unique and sometimes mysterious ways.

She told me, "My experiences involved butterflies. It was almost ridiculous. Butterflies followed me and appeared to me most days for a year following my son's death. Butterflies would come to my window, find their way inside my car, and encircle me."

On one day, when it was freezing outside, Janene thought, *Well, I won't see a butterfly today.* But soon, she opened an art book to a photograph of a beautiful monarch butterfly waiting for her inside the pages.

In the Christian tradition, butterflies are a symbol of resurrection and transformation. For Janene, the butterflies brought comfort.

I also asked Janene if she had ever experienced the Lord's touch on her shoulder as I had. She said, "No, just the movement of air and an undeniable presence."

A neighbor of ours in the Hill Country told his story to my husband and me. Ken had married a woman of Indian heritage, eventually bringing three children into the world together. Their son P. J. was killed instantly in an automobile accident. P. J. and his brother, Jim, were not on good terms at the time of his death. As Ken told it:

After P. J.'s death, Jim suffered severely due to the broken relationship and the lost opportunity for

repair. He began to drink heavily and entered rehab
several times. He later stayed in a halfway house
with just four or five other people. They cooked for
themselves and had professionals come in to work
with them. One of these people was an Indian,
and part of his ritual with my son (since he was
also of Indian descent) was to send him out on the
mountain to watch the sun come up.

One morning, as the sun was rising, Jim saw an
eagle feather fall from the sky. He felt it was a sign
from God that his brother forgave him and was
letting him know that all was well with him. If that
hadn't happened, I don't know where my Jim would
be today.

God comforted Jim in the way that he needed at that time.
One of my close friends lost her brother in a truck accident
years before. Speaking to the deceased man's mother, Ruth, I
asked if she'd had any extraordinary experiences with the Lord
after the death of her son, John. She told me:

Yes, I did have experiences, but I don't tell anybody
about these things because people might wonder
about my mental stability or think I just imagined
things. But you have lost children, so I'll tell you.

I always sat at the end of the row in church,
leaving a spot for Van [her husband], who was a
greeter and would come in late.

Sitting in church one day, the knife of grief was plunging right through me. I couldn't bear the pain. Then I heard a voice saying, 'Hello, my name is John. Can I sit with you?' And I looked up to see a young man with brunette hair—the same hair color and similar to my John. He sat down beside me. My pain disappeared, and I was at peace. He never spoke again, but he didn't need to. We sat in communion through the service, and he quietly left. I knew I had been in the presence of an angel.

In his book *Telling Secrets*, Frederick Buechner tells of an experience of God's presence in his life. It occurred during his darkest days when he was dealing with his daughter's anorexia (which would later take her life). He had stopped his car on the side of the road, lost in despair. A car appeared with a personalized license plate that spelled out T-R-U-S-T. Buechner realized it could be considered the kind of joke life sometimes plays on us, but he acknowledges it as something else. Something more. It was "the one word out of all the words in the dictionary that I most needed to see exactly then."[17] He recognized it as a word from God.

As I have spoken with dozens of grieving parents, I have realized that not all of them have had extraordinary comforting experiences. Most had comfort that came in more conventional ways. When losing our two sons, the Lord spoke to my heart and brought comfort from far and wide through people, but there was no experience of His presence the way He came the third time.

A Portrait of Grief

In the song for today, Larry Fleet says that he finds God "in the kindness of strangers, the quiet of the water, in a deer stand or a hayfield," whether he's looking for Him or not. To process and move through devastating loss, sometimes we need Jesus to touch us. We need Him to tenderly mend our broken hearts. He is free to do that in whatever way He chooses. He can do it through the words and deeds of others. He can bring comfort through His written words or through the beauty of His creation. But we must be open to looking for Him in the midst of our pain. If we perceive Him to be distant and uncaring, it will be more difficult for us to recognize and receive His presence. If, however, we discover that He is with us in our suffering, we are more able to accept the comfort and assurance He offers.

I read in the book of Exodus:

> Now Moses was pasturing the flock of his father-in-law, Jethro, the priest of Midian; and he led the flock to the west side of the wilderness and came to Horeb, the mountain of God. Then the angel of the LORD appeared to him in a blazing fire from the midst of a bush; and he looked, and behold, the bush was burning with fire, yet the bush was not being consumed.
>
> — Exodus 3:1–2

And in the Book of Daniel, King Darius speaks of the God of Daniel: "He rescues, saves, and performs signs and miracles in heaven and on earth, He who has also rescued Daniel from the power of the lions" (Daniel 6:27).

I'm no Moses, and I'm no Daniel. But I am no less a child of the living God. Why shouldn't He appear to me or to you?

The Lord most always arrives unexpectedly—unexpected like a burning bush, a parted sea, a virgin birth, a suffering Savior, or a risen Lord. I'm learning to expect the Lord to do the unexpected in my life. I look for Him to appear in my everyday life through circumstances, through people, and, yes, through the miraculous. Why not? We serve a risen Lord. He is in the world. As J. I. Packer says, "The victim of Calvary is loose and at large." We are free to experience Him as powerfully as did His disciples. No, we can't see Him as they did, but oh, my friend, He sees me, and He sees you! He walks with me and talks with me. Why can't He touch me or you?

You may say, "Really, Cheryl? Red birds, butterflies, and angels? I just can't believe all that!" To that statement, I can only say *it is the truth.*

Perhaps the real question is, do we recognize our moments of visitation? Or do we dismiss them as fantasy or delusion? In Luke 2:19, we are told that Jesus wept over Jerusalem because its' people did not recognize their moment of visitation from God. Wisdom comes not in always questioning His appearing but in being alert to His appearing. We can recognize them by the burning of our hearts and the lifting of our spirits.

I've noticed that God likes to show up in the small, the hidden, and the ordinary things of life. Yes, He can send a message through a red bird, a butterfly, a warm touch, an eagle's feather, or even a baby wrapped in swaddling clothes. The primary reality of the Lord's messages to us, the broken-hearted, is to reveal to us the truth of His goodness. He sends us messages and speaks to us out of the richness of His love, offering us a sense of its depth. He draws near to bind up our broken hearts. He whispers to us the reality of the marvelous and the mystery of life everlasting. We are not to lose hope.

When in deepest anguish, it is not wrong to ask for God's assurances that He is still in control and that our loved ones are secure. We are, however, cautioned in Scripture not to seek reunion with the dead through spiritists or mediums. As we read, "Let no one be found among you…who practices divination or sorcery, interprets omens, engages in witchcraft, or casts spells, or who is a medium or spiritist or who consults the dead. Anyone who does these things is detestable to the Lord" (Deuteronomy 18:10b–12, NIV).

All the signs, epiphanies, and everyday miracles I have mentioned here gave birth to a deep hope within for those gifted by them. Our Lord knows our frame. He knows how we are made and what we need. True faith believes without seeing, however sometimes God, in His compassion, sends those who believe something to see.

As the Psalmist tells us, "*I had fainted*, unless I had believed to see the goodness of the LORD in the land of the living" (Psalm 27:13, KJV).

Prayer for Today

Oh, Lord, open my eyes to see You. Come, Holy Spirit, come. Come in any way You choose, just don't let me miss Your appearing to me. Teach me Your wisdom that is learned only through the pain of love. In the name of Jesus, Amen.

PART THREE

Special Needs

CHAPTER FOURTEEN

Loss of Identity: During Grief, We Ask, "Who Am I Now?"

"Know that the LORD Himself is God; It is He who has made us, and not we ourselves; *We are* His people and the sheep of His pasture."

— Psalm 100:3

SONG TO HEAL YOUR HEART

"You Say" by Lauren Daigle

Amid such tremendous loss and suffering, I lost sight of who I was.

I had been a mother with a child at home since I was twenty-one. With the loss of our youngest son, three months short of his 17th birthday, we had an empty nest. It was not the typical empty nest that most parents experience. Ours was suddenly, unexpectedly, and permanently empty. I found myself at a terrible loss of meaning.

It is said that nature abhors a vacuum. And I was empty. I had a severe case of, "Who am I now?"

My husband and I had always worked together. When I went into the studio now, I could not breathe and stopped going to work. Our work took us into the public eye constantly. After that second year, I started running around in circles, trying to fill the void with extreme busyness. It seemed impossible for life to continue the way it had always been.

Running miserably from vocation to vocation, from city to city, from country to country, from adventure to adventure, I attempted to fill my emptiness and create a new world and a new identity. For some unknown reason, it felt good to be with strangers and in strange places. Distraction has its uses in desperate times.

After experimenting in several work settings involving fashion, marketing, and etiquette, I enrolled in a fashion course at the Paris American Academy in France. The head of the school, whom I had met on a previous group trip, introduced me to new and experienced designers. To my great surprise, several of the designers spoke to me about putting together a collaboration to create a fashion line for America.

After returning home and conducting extensive research, I decided to enter the international bridal market in collaboration with a French designer of gowns and an English designer of hats and veils. It soon became obvious that it was going to be a very expensive endeavor. Neither of the other designers had money to put into the venture, just talent. With a homemade business plan to raise money, eleven local investors came on board, and we started a bridal gown business called Christopher & LaLou.

For five years, I traveled from Beaumont to New York and to Paris regularly, creating and selling bridal gowns. Along with our regular line, we designed a small collection of gowns embellished with the Lalique muguet crystals. The French crystal company, Lalique, debuted our gowns in their boutique in New York. We had multiple editorials and covers in national bridal magazines. One of our designs was selected as the logo gown for the first March on Madison by the Conde Nast Magazine Group. Lalique had plans to debut our gowns in their boutiques in the Middle East and in Japan, and we had nine boutiques in the States along with an exclusive with Saks Fifth Avenue for the Lalique Collection.

We sold dresses and had much success, but not enough. We were running out of money. All the while, I solicited more funds from my original investors and new investors, but the money did not come in time. With the euro soaring and the dollar losing value, we were paying too much to make the gowns.

I was finally forced to close the business. It was a sad ending.

My husband had put up with my frantic projects and my frenetic running to and fro across the earth. I know it was hard for him. We had always worked together, played together, and raised our children together. I realized then that nothing could really fill the void created when losing our child. I had chased around the world looking for me. I had searched the eyes of strangers to see if they knew who I was. I had looked in all the wrong places, and I finally came limping home.

Three months after closing the bridal business, our oldest son, Wes, took his life. And everything stopped. Wes' absence spoke more loudly than any presence—and everything lost its meaning. I could relate to the following poem, *pieces*, by Jim Branch.

a piece at a time is how it comes
and where
does

                    it

                                all

              fit?
and how?

can i see the picture again? so i'll know,
if not i'll have no clue of where each one fits.   or me.
making sense of the pieces
without the picture

                            seems an impossible task
false assumptions
                rabbit trails
                                wrong turns
now i see it
no i don't

waiting…
        for the next piece to be given
waiting…
for all to fall into place   in time
doubting…
            in the midst of the jumble
can i see the picture again? so i'll know.

i need to know to my depths the beauty of it all
i need to know the beauty of the pieces   and trust
because a piece at a time is how it comes[18]

The loss of a child strikes at the core of who we are. It is as if a part of us has been stolen. The whole world changes, as does every relationship and every aspect of our lives. The changes keep piling up. Instinctively, we know we will never be the same. What do we do with all of this? The loss of a child saps the meaning from every pleasure and the satisfaction from every accomplishment. We become like robots, going through the motions. I've learned it doesn't really matter if one is in Texas or New York, or France; the anguish, emptiness, and lostness are still there.

And again, the questions rise up: Did I miss something the first time around, Lord? What are You doing? Have You abandoned us? What do You want from me? Who am I anyway? Does it even matter?

As pastor Lloyd J. Ogilvie says, "When the night of suffering comes with its stark reality, there is no alternative [but to bear it]. And then we are faced with the ultimate temptation—to make God our adversary and not our advocate. We say with the psalmist, 'Why has thou forgotten me?' That's the dark night of the soul."[19]

Often, as mourners, we are tempted to see God as our adversary, plotting evil against us. But we know it isn't true. We are the objects of His love, and we must at some point surrender even our questioning to Him.

If you have ever been to Italy, you may have seen Michelangelo's sculpture of David. This is considered one of the greatest works of art that exist. The statue was commissioned first in 1466 to be sculpted from a huge block of marble. Two artists had worked on it with no real progress. They both had pronounced the marble flawed, abandoning the project. The marble block lay neglected for twenty-five years in the courtyard of a Florence cathedral. Around 1500, when Michelangelo was twenty-six years old, he was contracted to sculpt David out of this piece of marble that was not only flawed but also weathered from exposure to the elements. It was said that he was unimpressed with the material he was given to work with, but it was too expensive and too valuable to be discarded.

When he looked at the block of marble, Michelangelo, the master sculptor, saw the figure of David within the stone looking back at him. As Michelangelo worked on the block of marble, chipping away the superfluous material, he had a vision, a purpose, and a plan. It was two years later that the masterpiece he imagined, and no one else saw, was revealed to the world. When asked how he did it, his response was, "It is easy. You just chip away the stone that doesn't look like David."

The Bible describes God as our maker and us as His masterpiece. The Apostle Paul tells us in his letter to the Ephesians, "For we are God's masterpiece" (Ephesians 2:10, NLT). When God wanted to illustrate what He was doing in our lives, He sent Jeremiah to a pottery studio to observe the potter. Watching, Jeremiah could see that the potter had complete power over the clay, just as Michelangelo did over the marble. We kid ourselves that we have control, that we can shape our own lives. When tragedy comes into our lives, we realize that not only have we lost control but that we never had it.

When suffering bears down, God is not playing with us. He is not cruel when He allows us to suffer.

As Lloyd J. Ogilvie says, "God does not send suffering. He doesn't have to. There's enough of it to go around in our weary world."[20]

But why is the world like this? Perhaps we should re-read Genesis. Aren't we the ones who shattered Paradise? We were given the power of choice. If we are honest, we can see that most of our suffering comes from human choice—either ours or someone else's. Our lives may be shattered, but God is not finished. He will use our sufferings as a tool to chip away the superfluous material from our lives, as Michelangelo did with his sculpture. God will make something beautiful of our lives if we will but yield to Him.

The teaching of Christ is true. As J. B. Phillips points out, "Our little life is acted against an immeasurable back-cloth of timeless existence... and if a man honestly opens his own personality to God, he will without any doubt receive something of the Spirit of God."[21] It is a paradox. As our own self is purified and heightened, we will come to bear a strong family likeness to Christ and yet be more "ourselves" than we ever were.

The world may seem to have no meaning. We may see no purpose in our lives. All may be confusion and uncertainty, but our Creator has a vision for us. He promises He has a purpose and declares He has a plan. As we read in Jeremiah 29:11, "'For I know the plans that I have for you,' declares the LORD, 'plans for prosperity and not for disaster, to give you a future and a hope.'"

Where does our true identity lie? Does it lie with our family, our friends, or our society? Does it lie in what we do? Does it lie in what we see when we look in a mirror? Does it lie in our accomplishments or in our investments? As hard as we try (and believe me, I tried hard), we cannot put meaning into our own lives through any of these pursuits. It is a job too big for us. Only almighty God can give meaning. I love Psalm 139:13–16, which says:

For You created my innermost parts;
You wove me in my mother's womb.
I will give thanks to You because I am awesomely
and wonderfully made;
Wonderful are Your works,
And my soul knows it very well.
My frame was not hidden from You.
When I was made in secret,
And skillfully formed in the depths of the earth;
Your eyes have seen my formless substance;
And in Your book were written
All the days that were ordained for me,
When as yet, there was not one of them.

You are not a mistake. You are not a misfit. You are fearfully and wonderfully made. After a loss like we have experienced, we tend to integrate our brokenness into our identity. God Almighty is the one who made us, who formed or, should I say, sculpted us. And He created us in His own image. He has ordained our destiny. He is the *only* one who has the right to tell us our identity.

In grief, the questions we ask are: Who am I? What am I worth? Where do I go from here? What is my destiny? All these questions are answered by our God.

Whatever has happened, no matter how empty we feel at the moment, our lives are in the process of being molded by the hands of a living Savior who promises to raise us to new life. As important as work is, creative expression is, accomplishments are, even children are—what is most important by far is God

A Portrait of Grief

calling us "loved, valued, accepted, forgiven sons and daughters of the King." You are divine royalty. Better than that, you're a joint heir with Jesus.

I have finally learned that our identity can only be *bestowed*. And I agree with Jim Branch, who says,

> So much challenge, each and every day is to stop the ongoing patter of trying, in desperation, to create a self that has in fact *already been fearfully and wonderfully made*; and to simply receive my true self in peace and in freedom from the God who made me uniquely and loves me dearly. It is funny how much I strive to make a name for myself when only he can give me the name I was made to bear—my true name.[22]

You have value. You have meaning. You have worth.

You have all these qualities because the Master Sculptor, the King of Kings, has bestowed them upon you.

Prayer for Today

Oh, Lord, I've lost more than my child. I've lost myself as well. I've looked for my meaning and identity in many places, in many ways. I'm so tired. Set me free from my striving. Help me to rest and wait upon you for a while longer. I want to rest in Your arms. I want to hear Your words of love spoken to my heart. Give me a vision for the future, Lord, for without one, I will surely die. Help me to wait for You to bestow the identity, the purpose, and the name I was created for. Amen.

A Portrait of Grief

CHAPTER FIFTEEN

Marriage Amid Misery: Can We Make It?

"And He answered and said 'Have you not read that He who created them from the beginning made them male and female,' and said, 'for this reason a man shall leave his father and his mother, and be joined to his wife; and the two, shall become one flesh?' So they are no longer two, but one flesh. Therefore, what God has joined together, no person is to separate."

— Matthew 19:4–6

SONG TO HEAL YOUR HEART

"Remember When" by Alan Jackson

When friends gathered at our home after Austin's death, one couple came through the receiving line loaded with books on grief. Several years earlier, they had lost a son on the same dangerous road where our son had died.

"You *will* get a divorce!" the woman prophesied. "The statistics all say your marriage can't survive the loss of a child."

Our son Monty, standing next to me, leaned over and inquired, "Do you want me to punch her, Mom?"

While it is true that grief complicates, catastrophic loss is not necessarily a death sentence to your marriage. Statistically, the divorce rate among grieving parents is not so bad.

In 2006, The Compassionate Friends organization commissioned a survey of parents who had lost a child, with one question focusing on divorce. The poll found that only 16 percent of the parents divorce after the death of a child.

When people congratulate my husband and me on our long marriage or when the conversation turns to divorce, my husband and I say, "We both wanted a divorce—just never at the same time." That statement always brings a laugh. But it is true.

Three years after our fourth child, Austin, was born, Gary told me, "Although I know you are the prettiest and the best for me, I don't love you anymore." He wanted out.

In shock, I asked him to pray with me. We knelt by our bedside and prayed for God to heal our marriage. Getting up, I went for a walk to discuss this new revelation with the Lord.

Through tears, I cried to the Lord, "Father, you know my lifelong request has been that I would have a family that loved you and loved one another. But here we go again. If this is what You want for me, then somehow, I know it will be okay, but You must promise to stay close to me. I can't do this alone."

Then Bill Glass came to town. Bill was an outstanding former NFL defensive end who played eleven seasons, beginning with the Detroit Lions and finishing his career as a standout with the Cleveland Browns. Bill spent several off-seasons attending Southwestern Seminary, and Rev. Billy Graham encouraged him toward a life in the ministry. Founding Bill Glass Ministries, he led evangelistic crusades around the country and started a prison ministry.

We learned that a Bill Glass citywide crusade would be coming to Beaumont. Gary was a deacon in our church and a member of the steering committee to bring the city together for the crusade. For the next two weeks after our talk of divorce, Gary attended spiritual rallies and small prayer groups with Bill Glass. Bill trained a group of counselors, including Gary, to lead others to Christ.

Gary sat with the other leaders behind Bill on the stage as he delivered the messages to a packed auditorium for the next week. On the last night of the crusade, my husband got up at the end and went down to the front. I assumed he was going to counsel someone. When I went to the back where the counseling was taking place, peering through the window into the counseling room, I saw my husband on his knees with another counselor speaking to him.

My heart began to pound as I paced the hall. I felt like I was awaiting a birth. I discovered what I hoped for was true. Gary had gone to the counseling room for himself. He said he had been christened, baptized, and "deaconized" but had never surrendered his life to Jesus. He surrendered that night.

He was truly born again, a new person. He set about reordering his life and turning back toward us.

And did we live happily ever after? No, that's not life in this world. But we did have many, many good times before tragedy came calling.

I tell you this to confirm what most people already know: marriage is hard, even in good times. When the world we inhabit is upended by the violent convulsion of a child's death, the atmosphere fills with anger, irritability, and frustration. This anguish often separates us from those closest. What we yearn for can't be found in one another. It is as though the family dynamic must be redesigned and recreated, for it can never be the same. When our youngest and only child still living at home vanished from our lives, there was a void that could not be filled. An empty space lay between my husband and me.

I wanted a divorce after Austin died. I couldn't stand for life to go on the way it would have had he lived, and I wanted to change everything.

Gary wanted a divorce after the death of our oldest son, Wes.

Some think the death of an older child who is living independently is easier than the death of a younger child still in the home. I would say neither is easier; they are only different. The one thing that made Austin's death so hard for me was the absence of his physical presence, which I was accustomed to each day. So many daily tasks of caring and relating were gone. His daily need for food, transportation, appointments, and a thousand other details were missing from our lives. With Wes, I was not expecting to see him daily. He no longer depended upon us for all his needs. Although the loss was as great, the grieving was different. After Wes's death, lunch meat and instant oatmeal didn't break my heart as it did with Austin.

Although the changes at home were less than with Austin, our marriage began to unravel in a serious way after Wes's death. This might have been because it was the second time around with grief, and we couldn't bear to imagine getting through the suffering again. Maybe it was the anger, guilt, and confusion that come about in surviving a child's suicide. Whatever the reasons, we felt the need to separate. We each had to decide whether there was enough left to rebuild upon; the brokenness and disappointment were so great.

Even after going through this before, the grief and the mourning were different this time. As each child is different, so is the loss of each child. It is like a whole new experience. We also discovered that grief awakens grief. At times I didn't know which boy I was mourning over. We still had a lot to learn about grieving together separately.

Around this time, I found inspiration in the wonderful children's book *Tear Soup* by Pat Schwiebert and Chuck DeKlyen. The book describes an older couple, Grandy and Pops, who has suffered a terrible loss. The book suggests that Grandy and Pops must each individually and carefully prepare a big pot of tear soup, combining all the memories, misgivings, feelings, and tears. It had to be eaten slowly over a long period of time. Grandy and Pops had been married for many years, and they knew each individual pot of tear soup had to be prepared alone and with different ingredients even though they suffered the same loss. There is a lot of wisdom in that little book.

We learned that our marriage was not able to meet all our needs. We couldn't help one another, as the loss simultaneously ripped each of us apart. Grief demands so much energy and leaves little to give to another. While the expectation is to support our spouse, profound isolation is often the reality. We are so self-absorbed there is nothing to give. The grieving is different in men and women. That can complicate the situation further. Women tend to be more vocal, men more subdued or private or full of action. The very difference can lead to misunderstanding and accusations.

Because marriage is designed by God to be other-centered, a long period of selfish self-care is not ideal for marriage stability.

We couldn't help one another this second time around, and our capacity for self-deceit can make us believe all the problems lie in our mate.

We separated after Wes's death. I wonder if we just needed to change the subject from grief to something, anything else. We began to focus on our dissatisfaction with each other instead of the misery we were enduring.

Thoughts of divorce did not come easily for us. As Christians, we knew that God had designed marriage to be a picture of His covenant relationship with His people. We knew we were bound to obey the Lord's command to illustrate the glorious love of Christ for His church through our story. But our story was so broken and hopeless. How could we go on? Where was the hope? What was the purpose?

Determined to try as hard as we could, we started marital counseling. If we were to survive as a couple, we needed the Spirit of God to soften our hearts, which were quickly hardening toward one another. Although we were tempted to abandon one another in an attempt to escape the misery we were living in, we chose to trust God to sustain us.

There was so much anger, not directed at God this time, but rather at one another. We learned, despite everything, to express our anger out loud, to forgive, and to move on. We learned to let go of unrealistic expectations. We learned to respect the other person's moods and tried to refrain from mind reading. We learned it is best to ask, "How are you feeling? What are you thinking?" We learned just to listen, not to try to fix anything.

We learned to speak our needs to one another. "I need to be alone. I need to be held. I need time with you."

We refused to shy away from touching. We made a greater effort to be kind, patient, thoughtful, and forgiving. We focused on each other's strengths and tried to encourage instead of criticize. We prayed for restoration. We wrote each other notes to explain what could not be spoken. Gary bought me flowers. We tried to focus on ourselves, each other, our living kids, and our growing number of grandchildren. We learned to think of the good things in our life, and not on what could have been or might be coming. It was really hard. And it was worth the effort.

Because grief is both physically and emotionally exhausting, some people admit they just don't have the energy to make their marriage work. That doesn't mean the love is gone, only the energy. But know this: your marriage can survive.

In *The Fault in Our Stars*, John Green explains how the pleasure of remembering can be taken away "because there was no longer anyone to remember with. It felt like losing your co-rememberer meant losing the memory itself as if the things we'd done were less real and important than they had been hours before."[23] There is great comfort in having someone who shares your memories. I can't imagine losing that. There is an intimacy in shared history and in simply being understood.

I am grateful to still have someone to remember with. My husband and I still share our sadness over our missing children, but we also share wonderful memories of all our children. We have grown in oneness again, and together we pray that our marriage is becoming not just an "us story" but a gospel story of redemption. Yours can too.

Prayer for Today

Father, fill us with a passion for You, a passion for life, and a passion for one another. Through the power of Your Spirit, breathe life into our marriage. Help us to navigate these pain-filled days and to emerge more like you. We ask in the name of Jesus. Amen.

CHAPTER SIXTEEN

Suicide, the Ultimate Tragedy: The Aftermath Leads to a Prevailing Question—Why?

"It is because of the Lord's loving kindnesses that we are not consumed, Because his [tender] compassions never fail. They are new every morning; Great and beyond measure is your faithfulness."

— Lamentations 3:22–23, AMP

SONG TO HEAL YOUR HEART

"Show the Way" by David Wilcox

There is probably no greater nightmare than losing a child to suicide. As parents, we believe our job is to support our children, care for them, make them happy, and make their lives good. Suicide makes us feel like failures in this most important job of our lives.

When I was growing up, I never heard the word *suicide* spoken out loud. In those days, it was an unspeakable word, shrouded in taboo and mystery. It was a dark word, whispered in sentences that included other words like "unforgivable sin."

Although *suicide* is a terrible word, filled with stigma and shame, it can no longer be silenced or ignored. The suicide statistics in our nation place it among the leading causes of death. Sadly, suicide has become just another way to die.

Suicide bereavement, however, is distinct from other types of loss. When our son died by suicide, we felt guilty about something, but we weren't sure of our crime. We encountered shame and suspicion from a suicide death in the family that we had not experienced from any other loss.

Sometimes family members decide on a story to explain the death, attempting to avoid the accompanying stigma. Many suicides are explained away by saying they were accidents, such as accidental overdoses, accidental shootings, or accidental car wrecks. Although it is no one else's business whether a death is accidental or suicide, secrets are harmful to families. When the tragedy of suicide invaded our family, we were truthful from the beginning. Perhaps it was because our shock was so great that it never occurred to any of us to cover up the fact of suicide when our oldest son died.

Only in one situation did we withhold, but for a specific reason. Wes's boys were too young—at ages three, five, and eight—to understand what had happened, and my husband told them their dad had been cleaning a gun that misfired. Their mother told them the truth when they were older.

After losing our youngest child nine years earlier, we thought we knew all about grief. When our oldest son (and later our grandson) died by suicide, we found ourselves in a wilderness we had not experienced before. The "why" questions reverberated through our family like an atomic bomb.

With suicide, if you don't know why, you wonder what you missed, what you did wrong, and how you could have made things different. That occurs in all deaths, but it is so much worse with a suicide. There is a greater sense of responsibility.

For parents, suicide leaves us with a sense of abandonment. Secret suffering led to actions that we don't understand even years later and still can't believe our loved one was capable of. I felt bewildered, ashamed, and punished. Suicide is a loss that is earth-shattering. "The level of stress resulting from the suicide of a loved one is marked as catastrophic—equivalent to that of a concentration camp experience."[24]

We were spared the shock of discovering our son or witnessing his act. Others deal with images they will never forget. I was not spared my imaginings. A thousand times, I walked in our son's footsteps up the stairs to the room where he ended his life. It replayed in my mind like a movie on rewind.

In the past ten years, I have seen the stigma changing, possibly due to the increasing numbers of victims. When our dear Wes died, I felt like a failure as a parent. I noticed people avoiding me. I felt punished by God but wasn't sure why.

"Was our love not enough?" we asked ourselves and each other. Our surviving son kept asking, "Why didn't Wes call me?" Previously, they had called each other every day. Why not that day?

Tragically, Wes had tried to call his dad that day. Gary was on a photographic assignment and had turned off his phone. Our grandson, Brock, had reached out to his counselor in the rehab where he was living twice on the day of his suicide, telling her he was suicidal. She allowed him to go back to the dorm room, where he died.

Suicide is shrouded in mystery. Experts say those who complete suicide do so because of any number of reasons: mental illness, substance abuse, broken relationships, depression, or traumatic stress. Some choose suicide due to chronic pain, illness, or shame. Some fear becoming a burden to others. Surely, hopelessness must always enter into the decision-making.

But what causes one to choose suicide while others in the same situation do not? That is the mystery. Although suicide is at epidemic levels worldwide, little has been discovered to answer the vexing questions about why.

I can't claim to know what is going through any person's mind as plans are being laid to end one's life. It is a pretty sure bet that they can't believe they are valued and loved beyond measure. Somehow, they have lost their grip on that truth. Somehow, they have lost their way.

Ronald Rolheiser writes in the *Catholic Herald* that generally, when people die, it is against their will. It is no different when a death is from suicide except that the breakdown is spiritual and emotional and then lastly, physical. Suicide is not a cowardly or selfish sin but is instead an act of desperation, of surrender to a disease, or a deception that made living seem unbearable.

How, you ask, can a follower of Christ sink so low and be so confused to believe the lies of Satan and fall into so great a despair that they take their own life? To that, I would ask, how do any of us who follow Christ go on to commit adultery, lie, cheat, steal, or become addicted to alcohol, drugs, or pornography? Loneliness, grief, shame, and failure can take their toll on all of us. Don't we all lose our way at some point? Our hearts are a battlefield of faith versus doubt, the front line of the struggle between what is true and what is false.

But does the sin of suicide carry a sentence with it that is so grave as to keep one from the embrace of God? Does suicide dispense with it a card that reads, "Go directly to hell"? Is suicide an "unforgivable sin"?

I believe the answer is no.

Is suicide the greatest sin a person can commit? I can find no ranking of sins in my Bible. Some worry that with no time for repentance, the person who chooses suicide would enter eternity unforgiven. If this were true, would anyone be safe from condemnation? What if we were to die suddenly of heart failure or a car crash? We might have unconfessed sin in our life at the moment of death. Would Christ's atonement not be sufficient?

Often, our perspective of God is too small and too limited. We imagine Him snooping around, looking for a reason to punish and condemn. Our perspective of God should instead be big and unlimited. Over and over again in Scripture, God paints a portrait of Himself for us. He is the loving, grieving Father, running down the road to welcome His failure of a son who has finally come home. In the book of Hosea, God tells the prophet to take an unfaithful woman, a prostitute, for his wife as a picture of God's own relationship to unfaithful Israel. God stayed in a relationship with unfaithful Israel, never turning to the right or to the left. His love does not fail no matter how often we fail Him.

Over and over again, we watch Jesus as he pursues, forgives, and heals:

- "A bent reed he will not break off, and a dimly burning wick he will not extinguish" (Matthew 12:20).

- "For the death that he died, He died to sin [ending its power and paying the sinner's debt] once and for all" (Roman 6:10, AMP).
- "For by grace you have been saved, through faith, and this is not of yourselves, it is the gift of God" (Ephesians 2:8).

Surely God's compassion surrounds the depressed, the suffering, and the hopeless. Surely even for one who has rejected Christ all their lives, in the end, all of heaven bends low and listens closely to their final words, their final thoughts, to catch them calling His name, for that is all He needs. "Everyone who calls on the name of the Lord will be saved" (Romans 10:13). Jesus came to save, not to condemn. He is the Good Shepherd, looking for that one to the end.

In the face of the emotional and spiritual onslaught of suicide, the Gospel has a powerful counter-narrative to offer: each of us is made in God's image, we are loved more deeply than we can imagine, we are forgiven through our faith in Christ of each and every sin. Death will not ultimately triumph over life no matter how we die.

For those of us who survive a loved one's suicide, the aftermath is profound. In my case, the impact of suicide caused me to shut down. I cannot be specific about the events during this period, as I have blocked much of it out. I remember bits and pieces of the days before, during, and after the funeral, but very little. I was in a fog, emerging for moments and then back in the fog. Somehow, we got through it.

I didn't want to feel, so I went to sleep. In the beginning, I couldn't stand for anyone to look at me. I shut down my emotions and blocked out my thoughts for as long as possible while my husband went into overdrive. I lost my ability to do even the simplest of tasks. I only wanted to run as far away as possible from the overwhelming pain.

Several weeks after Wes's death, Gary got a call from his friend Judge Tom Mulvaney. Gary knew Tom through golf. We knew Tom had terminal cancer and had been praying for him before our world imploded again. He told my husband he wanted to come over to talk to me, saying he had a word from the Lord for me.

Tom had his wife drive him over and drop him off as he was no longer driving. He told me the story of his grandmother. "She was a beautiful woman," he said, "but my parents, my aunts, and my uncles always said, 'I wish you had known her before.'" Growing up, Tom never knew what that meant.

"When I was older," he continued, "I finally heard the story of what the 'before' was. Her oldest son had fought in World War II. When he came home, he wasn't the same. He was quiet and spent a lot of time in his room. Although he tried to get a job, nothing happened for him. My grandmother was the one that found him after he had hanged himself in his room. It was as if my grandmother died that day too. She was a shadow of herself. She never laughed again with the joy she had before. All of the color was drained out of her."

Tom concluded by saying, "Don't let that happen to you, Cheryl. Don't let this be your story. Grieve Wes, take your time about it, but don't stop living. The Lord sent me to tell you He wants you to live every moment that you are here on this earth. Please, don't give up now."

That day, as I looked into the eyes of a man who was fighting for his life with a terrible disease, I determined not to stop living while I was alive. I listened to the Lord's word that Tom brought to me. I would not give up. I chose to enter the darkness of mourning again, trusting God to lead the way. I set my intention on starting the journey. After all, our oldest son deserved to be mourned.

Don't let the story Tom told be your story either. Let's not let the story of our lives be written by tragedy and disaster. With God as our Father, we have the power to rise from the ashes and to live fully. We can choose life for ourselves. We can do and be what we wanted for our loved ones. We can be survivors. Let's hear the Lord's word that Tom brought to me that day: "Live! Don't stop living now. Please, don't give up now!"

Whatever you do, determine not to travel this path of healing alone. It is the hardest road imaginable. There is no consolation, no good, no positive sign to find in the circumstance. There have been so many things—too many things—left unsaid. There are so many questions left unanswered that, in the beginning, comfort is impossible. Even Bible promises that have been meaningful in the past and may be profoundly helpful in the future can be bitter in the beginning. We must choose not to give in to despair, and we can also encourage our loved ones to recommit to the gift of life that God has given each of us.

We are still here. We have been given the great gifts of life and time. My greatest wish for you, and for anyone grieving the terrible loss of suicide, is to allow the suffering to lead you to live more fully and to love more deeply than before. Fight for your own life the way you so desperately wish you could have fought for theirs.

Suicide seems to become the defining word for a person. Our son and our grandson were much more than the way they died. We remember each of them as the person they were and by the way they lived, not by the way they died.

Prayer for Today

Oh God, from whom nothing can ever separate us, my life is in Your hands. I can't see You or hear You today, but I know You are there. Help me to find a way to live again, for I ask in the name of the one who came that all might live anew. Amen.

CHAPTER SEVENTEEN

Complicated Grief: When Emotional Pain Turns Physical

"For we do not have a high priest who is unable to empathize with our weaknesses, but we have one who has been tempted in every way, just as we are—yet he did not sin. Let us then approach God's throne of grace with confidence, so that we may receive mercy and find grace to help us in our time of need."

— Hebrews 4:15–16, NIV

SONG TO HEAL YOUR HEART

"Truth I'm Standing On" by Leanna Crawford

I know what you are thinking when you see the title of this chapter. What grief *isn't* complicated? And it's true. All grief walks are complicated and difficult to navigate. Situations arise that demand intervention by counselors or experts, or physicians.

The Mayo Clinic website seems to indicate that grief is considered complicated when the normal stages continue for long periods of time or result in isolation, depression, or trouble functioning.

Some degree of depression, in my experience, is a normal response to the death of a child. In the second year of grieving our youngest son, I suddenly couldn't get out of bed or had difficulty doing so. It was impossible for me to decide what to wear for the day. Often my daughter would coach me through my wardrobe choices over the phone, suggesting what would be the appropriate clothing for the day.

I was seeing a counselor, who said she would not see me again until I called my doctor for antidepressants. She told me I had a clinical depression. The antidepressants helped—and I needed the help.

When traumatized by the loss of a loved one, mourners often replay the circumstances of the death again and again. While this may be a natural response, don't allow it to continue for too long before seeking help. After Austin's fatal car accident, I couldn't stop replaying the event as I envisioned it. The car he was in had hit a tree just off the highway. In my imagination, I was in the car and kept ramming into the tree over and over again. I lost control of my emotions, unable to stop crying. While it is normal to weep and healthy to do so, it is exhausting and cannot go on without a break.

My counselor used a therapeutic technique called Eye Movement Desensitization and Reprocessing (EMDR), which helped me move past experiencing the accident repeatedly. EMDR was quite new when my counselor used it to help me. It has become a widely used practice to help returning soldiers work through PTSD and others who have endured traumatic experiences.

A Portrait of Grief

The psychologist Francine Shapiro invented EMDR in the 1980s when she noticed that moving her eyes from side to side seemed to reduce the occurrence of her own distressing memories. Shapiro began studying psychology after being diagnosed with cancer. She is quoted as saying that her interest was in discovering the role of the mind in treating the immune system. Although the healthy mind and body connection had been well documented before, she wanted to liberate the mind from traumatic experiences. She noticed on a walk in the park that disturbing thoughts were less disturbing as she darted her eyes back and forth.

While talking and sobbing through what I was experiencing, my eyes followed my counselor's fingers from right to left. The purpose was to re-experience the trauma while giving words to it and to replace the memories that caused me to freeze in them with more tranquil thoughts. I didn't understand how it worked, but it did. Somehow, I became unstuck and was not doomed to the traumatic repetition.

A study by Gregory Nicosia helped people understand how EMDR works. Nicosia used brain mapping to demonstrate that brainwaves of the right and left brains are not synchronized after trauma. The research showed that EMDR enabled brainwaves in both sides of the brain to become more integrated and harmonized.

If you are stuck in traumatic imaging and unable to move forward, consider finding a psychologist or counselor certified in EMDR use. Some churches employ counselors trained in this practice.

Our daughter experienced a different kind of grief response after the first loss of a sibling. She began to lose consciousness when she exercised. She would feel dizzy and then wake up on the floor. It was particularly dangerous since she was a runner, often out alone or on a treadmill. She was diagnosed with cardiomyopathy and placed on medication, which she continued to take under the supervision of a cardiologist for several years. When she was ready to start a family, we visited a specialist, concerned about the stress pregnancy would put on her heart. The physician explained that she wouldn't know what would happen until she tried going off of the medication. She went off the medication and had no further issues, going on to have three healthy boys. Later her physician said it was most likely "broken heart syndrome," a temporary heart condition brought on by extreme stress.

My own response to grief was different after our grandson Brock's death. Perhaps there were no more tears to cry, or perhaps the Lord's preparation helped me through the funeral and the surrounding days. I don't know, but my emotions seemed pretty much controlled.

This time it was as though the grief attacked my body, a condition called somatization. According to the Kelty Mental Health Resource Center, "Somatization is the word we use for the physical expression of stress and emotions through the mind-body connections." There is constant communication between the brain and body, and all our emotions have physical connections. This connection is automatic and involuntary.

After Brock's death, I had a resurgence of the shingles, and my blood pressure soared. My cardiologist changed my medication again and again throughout the following year. He decided anxiety caused my blood pressure problems and asked me what was going on in my life. When he heard about Brock's death, he told me he could treat my blood pressure but could not treat grief and anxiety. He sent me back to my internist, who had sent me to him. She diagnosed me yet again with depression. At her recommendation, I started on antidepressants again and began going to a counselor for talk therapy.

I saw a Christian counselor following Brock's death who asked me to watch a video entitled "The Body Keeps Score," which explains EMDR more thoroughly. The video states that trauma rewires the brain and prevents us from living in the present.

While my new counselor did not use the standard EMDR techniques, he did something similar. He had me write out my traumas, and then immediately afterward, he wanted me to spend time painting at my easel. In doing these exercises, I was using my left brain to relive the trauma of losing Brock and using the creative part of my mind to process the event. In essence, I was swinging back and forth between using my left brain and right brain.

During that time, it was as though my heart and mind changed the subject from emotional distress to physical distress. I couldn't look to God while focusing on myself. Suffering does that. It can make us self-centered and self-absorbed. When you are already emotionally and physically exhausted from the pain of one loss, it can only help to seek support when more losses pile on.

Jay Adams says that grief tears life to shreds. He describes it as something that pulls a person loose and makes one come apart at the seams. Although Adams's words are true, remember the words of Jeremiah 30:17 (NIV): "'But I will restore you to health, and I will heal your wounds,' declares the LORD."

We know that suffering can never be completely removed on this earth. We await the new heaven and the new earth. Nothing can take away the grief you feel from losing a child or another you love and cherish, but therapeutic techniques and spiritual practices can relieve needless suffering.

In chapter 20, we will explore the power of prayer in more depth, but for now, let me just say this: the most healing activity you can engage in is prayer. If you think you don't know how to pray, dismiss that thought. Praying is simply talking to God. Tell Him you are afraid. Tell Him you are anxious. Ask Him to help you and to quiet your heart. He loves you and bends low to hear your words. Scripture tells us so: "Because he bends down to listen, I will pray as long as I have breath!" (Psalm 116:2, TLB).

Prayer for Today

God of all our days, these days are hard. I want to be better. Guide me as I seek healers for my mind and body. Lift up my head so that I can see You. In the name of Jesus, my healer. Amen.

PART FOUR

Finding Meaning

CHAPTER EIGHTEEN

Celebrating Those Lost Too Soon: Funerals, Memorials, and Other Tributes

"I thank my God in all my remembrance of you."

— Philippians 1:3

SONG TO HEAL YOUR HEART

"Thought About You" by Tim McGraw (Lyric Video)

The desire to be remembered lives within all of us. We write our names in fresh concrete on sidewalks and driveways. We carve our initials on trees. I wrote my children's names in the sand at the beach before they were born, taking photographs and placing them in their baby books. It is human to want to leave our mark, to be remembered.

For most parents, a primary legacy we leave behind in this world is our children. When we lose them early, we desperately want them to be remembered by others. Not just for them, but perhaps more importantly for ourselves.

I have planned funerals now for many people. A child's funeral is something we aren't prepared for. As with everything surrounding the death of our children, a funeral or memorial service seems so wrong and so jarringly out of place. We can lay our elderly loved ones in their graves with sorrow but also with gratitude for their contributions and accomplishments during their lifetimes.

To bury a child is something different altogether.

Fortunately, funerals provide some structure through which we can express our love publicly. There is a script to be followed, and that adds a perception of control. Often, we are in shock during the planning of the funeral. Attending the event can feel disorienting and surreal. Our friend John Wayland recently reminded me that when the limo pulled up in front of our house to take us to Austin's service, I said, "I'm sorry, Y'all. I'm not going. I don't want to go." But of course, I did go and was glad I did.

Different churches and different faiths may have variations in the way death is acknowledged and lives are celebrated. Any structure is helpful for grieving parents. Tradition and symbolism are useful in navigating through the devastating days following a death.

I had one Christian friend who, after losing her son, decided to follow many Jewish rituals to help her through the grief process. She had close Jewish friends who helped her step by step through the observances. For instance, she did not wear leather shoes when in deepest mourning. Wearing soft shoes during bereavement, she learned, is symbolic of personal mortification and a disregard of vanity and comfort in order better to concentrate on the deeper meaning of life. One of her Jewish friends brought her a black ribbon to wear during the thirty days of mourning. This is an expression of grief, as is the tearing of the clothes, indicating that a part of the grieving person has been torn away.

The music director from our church came to our home after Austin died to help us plan the funeral. I can remember saying, "John, this is Austin's every birthday celebration, his graduation from high school and college, his wedding celebration. It represents to me every joyful moment he has had, and every joyful moment he will never have." We carefully chose pictures and music that had meaning to him and for us. Although we needed to remember and reflect on his happy times and personal triumphs, we badly needed the service to point to the reality of the resurrection.

Let me encourage you to make the effort to create meaningful funeral arrangements—even though it is extremely painful to do so. Services of commemoration can give us solace and new memories to cling to. Funerals can strengthen our bonds with our family and with others. When leaving Austin's funeral, my eyes connected with others in the congregation that had lost their own children. I could feel their encouragement and support. Funerals give us an opportunity not only to express our love for our deceased children but also to give words to our faith. As grief counselor Dr. Alan Wolfelt says, "The best funerals remind us how we should live."

I have spoken previously of my trouble viewing the bodies of our children. If it is possible for you, summon the courage and strength to see your child's body. Doing so will help you accept the reality of the loss. Seeing them helps us to know that they are no longer present with us. As the Scripture tells us, "Then the dust will return to the earth as it was, and the spirit will return to God who gave it" (Ecclesiastes 12:7).

These days, the internet and social media have made planning a funeral and remembering a lost loved one easier. It is not necessary to rely totally on the newspaper to inform others of your loss. Obituaries and memorials are displayed online and shared through Facebook, Twitter, and other sites. Those who visit these sites can express their condolences and leave donations if they wish to. While flowers and personally expressed condolences and sympathy cards have remained popular, more families are requesting donations to charity to honor their loved ones.

It is no longer necessary for the expenses of a funeral to be a financial hardship. If you are struggling financially and the expense of a funeral is more than you can manage, consider a GoFundMe page. This is a crowdfunding platform that allows people to raise money for events, including funerals. (In addition to GoFundMe, other funding platforms are available.)

After our losses, we set up memorial funds so people could give a donation to a charity in lieu of flowers and gifts to our family. When Austin died, we set up a fund to support Young Life and one for the music ministry of our church. At Wes's death, we asked that donations go to an education fund for his three children.

With Austin in high school at the time of his death, his classmates found unique ways to memorialize him. The basketball team wore black patches on their uniforms with his initials embroidered on them. At the tree where he died, they set up an altar of Dr. Pepper bottles (in honor of his favorite soda). His school locker was stuffed with notes, and the locker was "retired."

We gave books to libraries with labels inside that read "In Memory of _____." We decorated our churches with flowers in their memories, usually at Easter. Our son wrote poems to honor his brothers. Many parents write books, either for publication or for family remembrance.

My father-in-law was a local politician in Beaumont. He was on the city council and later served as a county commissioner, initiating the construction of a new road to access our local university, Lamar, from Interstate 10. That street was named after him: Rolfe Christopher Drive. We had three oak trees planted on the boulevard—one in memory of each of our deceased sons and one for my husband's brother. (Both of my husband's two brothers, Craig and Todd Christopher, died of cancer in the same time period as our boys.) We placed memorial plaques beneath all the trees. We had steppingstones engraved with the names of all our children and grandchildren. Those steppingstones have traveled with us from home to home, from city to city, and now reside beneath a giant oak in front of our home in Bryan, Texas. There are stones engraved with their names at River Front Park in Beaumont, Texas.

I know two families who donated their children's organs to save others. What a wonderful living memorial to their children. It was a sacrificial and meaningful gift to both families and such a blessing to those who had loved ones saved by these gracious acts. This is possible only in special circumstances. None of our boys were organ donor candidates, not that it even occurred to me at the time.

Many parents use the tragedy in their own lives to improve the lives of others. Thirty-five years ago, Candy Lightner founded Mothers Against Drunk Driving after losing her thirteen-year-old daughter to a drunk driver. Not only did Candy change the attitude of Americans toward driving while intoxicated, but she also has undoubtedly saved many lives. I could not list the many parents who turned the deaths of their children into meaningful movements of influence and change.

Another way to keep your loved one's memory alive is through "in memoriam" scholarships. There is no time frame as to when memorials can be established. Some may do it immediately after the death; others take some years to take any action. This is your unique journey, so do it your way. Think about it and pray about it. You may ultimately choose to do nothing at all, and that is okay too.

One other thing is worth mentioning here. Memorabilia are objects kept or collected because of their history and the meaning we attach to them. At some point, you will need to deal with your child's belongings. When our children were alive, these things fell into the category of "stuff." After their death, they fall into a category labeled "precious." Since it is usually impractical to keep all their belongings, there are some questions we can ask ourselves to help decide what to keep:

- What is it about this keepsake that you selected to save? Usually, it is because we have an emotional attachment, but is it because it is valuable for another reason?
- Will this item be treasured by other family members as time goes on?
- Does this item represent something precious to your child, or does it represent memories of your child for you?

A Portrait of Grief

- Is this something you will look at every day? Will it make you happy or sad?
- Does the scent of the item remind you of happy times or sad times?

We kept many of Austin's shirts and sweatshirts because I wanted to wear them. I never wanted to wash them. We still have his favorite basketball shoes. We have golf clubs owned by Wes and Austin. For years I wore a silver locket with a photograph of Austin inside. Gary and I had given Brock a cross when he accepted Christ and was baptized. It was a retired cross that was no longer made. His mother had it copied, giving it to his two brothers and many of Brock's friends.

We attended a funeral a few years ago of an older friend, Doris. She loved scarves and had hundreds of them. The family had the scarves all spread out on tables and invited each person coming in to choose one of Doris's scarves to remember her. If your child has a collection that could be given away in that manner, this would be a way to memorialize your loved one.

Move slowly when it comes time to deal with your child's possessions. While in some ways it may seem silly to others, the things that touched them when they were alive have meaning to us as parents.

On a fundamental level, funerals, memorials, and memorabilia reinforce one central fact of our existence: we will die. Like living, dying is a natural and unavoidable process. Funerals help us search for meaning in the life and death of the person who died as well as in our own lives and impending deaths. Each funeral we attend serves as a sort of dress rehearsal for our own. Although funerals don't feel like opportunities, they do give us an opportunity to speak loudly about our values and beliefs about life and death and our love for those who have gone before us.

Prayer for Today

Lord, I can't help it—I hate death. I hate all that surrounds it. I hate parting. I love reunions and celebrations and champagne and dogs. I want life that never dies. I long for sunshine that doesn't dim, for happy days that never end in sadness. I yearn for joyful music that never stops, for flowers that never fade, for healthy bodies that don't get sick. Please come soon. I love the good that this world offers, but it is not enough. I long for life and love that never dies. I long for You. Come, Lord Jesus, come. Amen.

CHAPTER NINETEEN

Shaping Our Worries into Prayers: Though God Seems Silent, He Listens Closely to Our Heartfelt Words

"Do not be anxious about anything, but in everything by prayer and pleading with thanksgiving let your requests be made known to God. And the peace of God, which surpasses all comprehension, will guard your hearts and minds in Christ Jesus."

— Philippians 4:6–7

SONG TO HEAL YOUR HEART

"God Who Moves The Mountains"
(Lyric Video) by Corey Voss

Why?

Why pray?

Why pray now?

Why pray now when your prayer has gone unanswered?

There are many ways I failed as a mother and a grand-mother, but *not* praying for my children and grandchildren is *not* one of them. I prayed and prayed and prayed. I prayed with them, over them, and for them. I knocked on the door of heaven day after day, year after year, with petitions for those I loved. And I have seen answered prayer—miraculous answers to prayers. It is undeniable that God often spoke healing and hope into my life and the lives of those closest to me.

But then *the* prayer for the safety of our children, he did not answer—at least not in any way I could accept.

After the death of each of my dear family members, for the most part, I went silent. My prayers ceased.

The Christian life is not so much about doing good deeds and obeying rules as it is about a relationship. As in any close relationship, our faith in Christ depends upon trust. As flawed, sinful people, we fail in our faithfulness to God daily. When we perceive that God has broken the trust and failed us, we have a big problem with Him. As in any other relationship, it takes time for trust to be rebuilt.

When totally devastated and disappointed with the Lord, many speak of the absence of God. Often those of us who think we have a solid faith built on rock find new feelings of doubt and anger rising up within. The sturdy foundation that once held us firm becomes shifting sand, unsteady and unreliable.

After C. S. Lewis lost his wife to cancer, he questioned even God's reality. He wrote:

> Meanwhile, where is God? This is one of the most
> disquieting symptoms… go to him when your need
> is desperate, when all other help is vain, and what

do you find? A door slammed in our face and a sound of bolting and double-bolting on the inside. After that, silence. You may as well turn away. The longer you wait, the more emphatic the silence will become. There are no lights in the windows. It might be an empty house. Was it ever inhabited?[25]

While I never experienced the total absence of God that many feel, I did experience feelings of betrayal. Why didn't He save my boys? Where was He when I needed him most? What became of all of those promises for safety and protection? While I wavered in my trust and doubted His love, there was never a moment when I did not know that God was present. I diverted my eyes from Him and ran away from Him, but I was always aware of His watchful eye over me—for I had experienced Him as the God who "sees me" (Genesis 16:13).

When living in the shadow of unanswered prayer, it is easy to wonder if God has stopped caring for us. It is particularly maddening to hear that He is listening to others and granting their requests. Does God play favorites? Did He protect other people's children but not mine?

After losing a child, it distressed me to hear stories about others' answers to prayer. In a Bible study group not long after losing our youngest son, a woman shared her answered prayer. She was having a big party in her home and the day brought in a rainstorm that only Southeast Texans know about. We call it a "gully washer," which can go on for days. She prayed and stood on God's promises, asking Him to stop the downpour that threatened her party.

"An hour before the party," she boasted, "the Lord parted the dark skies, the rain stopped, and the sun came beaming through, just in time." Her guests walked into her home on dry land.

My heart cried out, "How, Lord, can You answer her prayer to save her party yet not save my son? What am I to do with that?"

Although she was my friend, I was appalled to discover that I really wanted to hear that it rained buckets, drenching all the guests, soaking the food, and blowing over the rented tent. Am I so petty to have wished for that? Or a wounded soul desperately searching for answers and reassurance from God?

One friend began to send me emails telling me of answers to prayers in the lives of people he knew. I know it was his attempt to rebuild my flagging trust in God, but it only made me angry. He told me of healings. He told me of children saved from possible disaster. He told me of a couple who had been praying for years to become pregnant and just got word that they were expecting. I didn't want to hear any of this. Finally, I asked my friend to please stop sending me these emails. I told him, "Just send me the stories of those who prayed for things and never got them. How did they react then? Did it affect their marriage? How did it affect their faith? Could they still pray? Did they praise God anyway? Did they experience the 'peace that passes all understanding'?"

When sorrow is heaped upon sorrow, we cannot help but wonder if the Lord has turned against us. As darkness closes around us in the death of our loves, we are sent on a pilgrimage that can end in a heart turned to stone. It is the unanswered prayers that hurt the most. I admire Tony Evans, pastor of Oak Cliff Bible Fellowship in Dallas. When Tony's wife, Lois, became ill with cancer, he not only prayed for her healing, but he also asked his church and the nation to pray for her healing.

At his wife's funeral, Tony asked their son, Jonathan, to deliver a eulogy. In this powerful tribute, Jonathan answers some of our questions about prayer in the face of death in his eulogy for his mother. In the eulogy, Jonathan said:

I was wrestling with God because I said, 'If we have victory in Your name, didn't You hear us when we were praying? Didn't You see the cancer?... Didn't You hear us? Why didn't You do what we were asking of You?' Because your Word says, 'If we abide in You and Your Word abides in us we can ask whatever we will and it will be given to us?' Your Word tells us that if we ask according to Your will that You hear us.

Your Word is telling us in Mark 11 that 'if you pray believing you will receive.' 'To be anxious for nothing, but through prayer and supplication make your request known.' 'Where are You?'

I was wrestling with God the last few days because this was a great opportunity that we can tangibly see Your glory.

Everybody was praying, not only in Dallas, but around the country and around the world. People were watching. Where are You? This was an opportunity to see Your glory.

And as I was wrestling with God, He answered.

And He said, 'Number 1, You don't understand the nature of My victory because just because I didn't answer your prayer your way doesn't mean that I haven't already answered your prayer anyway.'

'Because victory was already given to your mom. You don't understand because of the victory that I have given you.'

'There was always only two answers to your prayers—either she was going to be healed or she was going to be healed. Either she was going to live or she was going to live. Either she was going to be with family or she was going to be with family. Either she was going to be well taken care of or she was going to be well taken care of. Victory belongs to Me because of what I've already done for you.

The two answers to your prayer are yes and yes. Because victory belongs to Jesus.'

Then He said to me, 'You need to understand that I am God and I am sovereign. And My game plan is bigger than any one player on the field.'

'So you need to trust in the Lord with all your heart and do not lean on you, but lean on Me because I have the ability to make this crooked situation straight. I am the sovereign God. That's why they say that I am.'[26]

Even when it appears that God says no to our most meaningful and monumental requests, even during darkest grief, prayer can offer God's perspectives and shift our vision to the long game. Answers to prayer don't always come in "yes" or "no" responses. Our prayers are indeed answered, but often in ways we don't understand or see or hear. In my reading of Scripture, I noticed that Jesus never mentioned unanswered prayer. He said with certainty that *every* prayer is *always* answered. Jesus says, "Everyone that asks receives" (Matthew 7:8). I like his words to Jonathan Evans: "The answer was yes and yes."

Some revert to memorized prayers in time of need. That is fine and often meets a need, for death days are sacred and call out to us for sacred utterances. You will find many books that teach you how to pray. It is good to learn how to approach the Lord reverently. Of course, praise and thanksgiving are important, for they remind us of God's power and of our many blessings even now. I don't believe; however, the Lord waits for us to follow a form or to recite beautiful, memorized prayers when our need is urgent.

Be honest with God in your prayers. When we are ready to turn again to God for help, we must not be afraid to express our feelings. In most instances, especially in the lunacy of grief, we don't know what to say. We don't know what we need or how to pray, but we can pour out our feelings to the Lord. That's what the Book of the Psalms is—a pouring out of grief. If words fail you, pray the Psalms and remember that the Spirit prays for us, as we are told in Romans 8:26–27:

> The same way the Spirit also helps our weakness; for we do not know what to pray for as we should, but the Spirit Himself intercedes for us with groanings too deep for words; and He who searches the hearts knows what the mind of the Spirit is, because He intercedes for the saints according to the will of God.
>
> — Romans 8:26–27

We are told to pray in all things, the small and the great. We should never be afraid to pray for great things, for prayer puts us in touch with God's overcoming power. If we do not pray, God can do no great things in our lives. Frederick Buechner, in writing about prayer, spoke of the impact of Agnes Sanford on his life:

> [Sanford] said her idea of church was Jesus standing with his arms tied behind him, unable to give anybody anything because nobody dared ask him for anything, especially the minister, for fear that if the minister prayed for the healing of old Mrs. Smith, who is dying of lung cancer in the hospital and she wasn't healed, what would that do to his faith, and what will that do to the faith of the congregation? So the prayer is not prayed. [Agnes Sanford] said forget all that. Pray anyway. Pray anyway. Who knows what God can do through prayer?[27]

Prayer is personal. We are to come to Christ with our requests. He is concerned about everything that touches our lives.

Are you in pain? Pray for relief.

Are you in despair? Pray for comfort.

Are you hopeless? Pray for the Lord to fill your heart with hope.

Are you jealous of friends whose children are alive? Ask the Lord to change your heart.

We don't understand what has happened nor what is happening to us, but our help lies in the Lord. He wants to hear more than our requests. He wants to speak to us about our lives. As Lloyd J. Ogilvie says, "The purpose of prayer is not just to make the best of things, but to allow the Lord to use them to make the best of us."[28]

The rest and peace we long for never come from demanding answers and seeking understanding. Rest comes from reinvesting our trust in the one who knows all. As we wrestle with the Lord, prayer offers us a place to lay down our weapons. It is only in surrendering the anger and our need to know that we will find peace. Sooner or later, we must lay our loved ones before the Lord and surrender them into the arms of the One who is life.

With Lloyd Ogilvie, with Jonathan Evans, I will never again speak of "unanswered prayer." My prayers—and your prayers—are being answered in ways that we will one day understand and be amazed by.

Prayer for Today

Father, this is all so hard. I am so weak and so in need of You. Yet I fight You and Your will for my life. I talk back to You and stomp my foot like a foolish teen who wants her way. Forgive me. Teach me to love others the way You do. Soften my stony heart where it has become hard. I want to trust You again. Strengthen my faith and open my eyes to see life through Your eyes. Teach me to be kind and faithful and generous like Jesus, for I ask in His name. Amen.

CHAPTER TWENTY

Praise the Lord:
You May Not Feel Like It
But Try to Do It Anyway

"Even if the fig tree does not blossom, And there is
no fruit on the vines, If the yield of the olive fails,
And the fields produce no food, Even if the flock
disappears from the fold, And there be no cattle in
the stalls, Yet I will triumph in the LORD, I will
rejoice in the God of my salvation."

— Habakkuk 3:17–18

SONG TO HEAL YOUR HEART

"Even If" by Mercy Me

At our children's funerals, my husband and I stood and praised
the Lord in song, offering the sacrifice of praise. Our family and
the congregation joined us.

The Lord surrounded us, and many were brought to Christ
in those days.

After each death in our family, we were faced with unspeakable grief. There were many praise-less days, instead filled with distractions, bad choices, and suffering.

Years later, as we were emerging from the worst of our pain, Gary and I attended the funeral of a friend's wife. Neither of us knew Pam, only that she had endured a long battle with cancer.

Three of her girlfriends opened her service. They stood together at the front of the church and asked everyone in attendance to raise their right hand. And then one said, "Now keep your right hand in the air and raise your left hand. Now all together say, 'Praise the Lord.'"

Then the woman added, "That is what we witnessed Pam and her husband, Tris, do every day of her long battle with cancer."

When first diagnosed, "no matter the ups or the downs," Pam told her husband, "We will raise our hands to the Lord and praise Him every day." And they did, together, every day of her eight-year battle.

When she grew too weak to raise her arms, Tris would lift them up for her, and they would praise the Lord.

The Bible is full of examples of people who demonstrated their trust by the choices they made. The Book of Daniel is filled with lessons in trusting God.

After Israel was conquered by Babylon, three men named Shadrach, Meshach, and Abed-nego, along with their friend Daniel and 10,000 other Israelites, were taken as captives from Israel to Babylon. These outstanding four men were trained in the language and literature of Babylon so they could work for the king. The Old Testament account tells us that they had demonstrated a strong faith and trust in the Lord.

In Daniel 3, we read that King Nebuchadnezzar built a statue and commanded everyone to fall down and worship it—or else. The threat was real and demanded a choice. Fall down and worship the statue, or else suffer the consequences.

Doubt was cast upon the captive Jews by certain Chaldeans, who told the king that Shadrach, Meshach, and Abed-nego refused to bow down and worship the golden image. The king presented an ultimatum:

> Then Nebuchadnezzar, in rage and anger, gave orders to bring Shadrach, Meshach, and Abednego; then, these men were brought before the king. Nebuchadnezzar began speaking and said to them, "Is it true, Shadrach, Meshach, and Abednego, that you do not serve my gods, nor worship the golden statue that I have set up? Now if you are ready, at the moment you hear the sound of the horn, flute, lyre, trigon, psaltery and bagpipe, and all kinds of musical instruments, to fall down and worship the statue that I have made, very well. But if you do not worship, you will immediately be thrown into the midst of a furnace of blazing fire; and what god is there who can rescue you from my hands?

> — Daniel 3:13–15

They stood before Nebuchadnezzar, who possessed the power to kill them. He made a final offer: bow to my god this time, and you won't be burned alive. The three devout men made a bold response to the king:

> Nebuchadnezzar, we are not in need of an answer to give you concerning this matter. If it be so, our God whom we serve is able to rescue us from the furnace of blazing fire; and He will rescue us from your hand, O king. But even if He does not, let it be known to you, O king, that we are not going to serve your gods nor worship the golden statue that you have set up.
>
> — Daniel 3:16–18

Shadrach, Meshach, and Abed-nego trusted God, and no threat would sway them. It did not matter to them if they died that day. They feared the wrath of God more than the torture of a fiery furnace.

The king ordered them tied up and thrown into the furnace. Then the miracle happened: no burning men. Instead, Nebuchadnezzar, the great king himself, saw four men in the furnace walking around. And one of the four "looks like a son of the gods." Nebuchadnezzar was so amazed by what he witnessed that he exclaimed: "Blessed be the God of Shadrach, Meshach, and Abed-nego, who has sent His angel and rescued His servants, who put their trust in Him, violating the king's command, and surrendered their bodies rather than serve or worship any god except their own God" (Daniel 3:28).

Their decision to trust in the Lord showed Nebuchadnezzar that the one true God had real power. He was deeply impressed by their unshakable faith.

God is faithful, and therefore He is trustworthy. He is a solid foundation, not shaky ground.

And yet, sometimes—especially when personal tragedy strikes—we don't trust.

This is largely because we don't see the whole picture of our life like God does. Sometimes we see a "no" to our prayers as unfaithfulness on the part of God. Sometimes as our lives are unraveling before our very eyes, we feel abandoned by God.

He didn't rescue *our* children from the fire. He didn't keep *us* from the fiery furnace. God never said He would spare us from the fire, but He has promised to be present with us as He was with Shadrach, Meshach, and Abed-nego. Surely, He was also with our children.

We cannot see Him now, we cannot understand what is happening or what good can possibly come from our tragedy, but we know Him. We must believe and live Oswald Chambers' challenge to us: "Faith is the heroic effort of your life. You fling yourself in reckless confidence on God."

As you pass through the fire right now, there may be extremely difficult days behind and ahead—remember, God is with you, just as He stood in the midst of the furnace with Shadrach, Meshach, and Abed-nego. If we stand for God, He will be glorified through our decision.

Just as in the days of Shadrach, Meshach, and Abed-nego, the world is looking for living proof. Living proof that God is who He says He is, that He will do what He says He will do. That is who we are, the proof, the living proof.

Pam Cattan, the woman who praised God throughout her cancer ordeal, died, but she didn't lose her battle. God did not spare her the fire of the furnace. But she gave testimony every day of His presence in the flames. With Paul, she fought the good fight; she finished the race, she kept the faith. Well done.

Pam lived out the admonition of the Apostle Paul: "Fight the good fight of the faith; take hold of the eternal life to which you were called and for which you made the good confession in the presence of many witnesses" (1 Timothy 6:12).

May we all be so bold, courageous, and trusting.

Prayer for Today

Oh Lord Jesus, when in the fiery furnace, give us vision to see You. Fill our hearts and our mouths with the sacrifice of praise. Give us faith to trust You even if You don't do as we ask. We hope in You alone. Amen.

CHAPTER TWENTY-ONE

The Impossible Promise of Romans 8:28: What Good Can Possibly Come of This?

"And we know that God causes all things to work together for good to those who love God, to those who are called according to his purpose."

— Romans 8:28

SONG TO HEAL YOUR HEART

"Way Maker" (Live from Passion 2020) by Kristian Stanfill, Kari Jobe, and Cody Carnes

All things are not good. The death of our children is not a good thing. Illness, accidents, betrayals, discouragement, depression, drug addiction, are not good things. But the Bible tells us that God is working it out. More than that, "He is working it out for good."

From the time I became a believer at age twelve and began to read my Bible, Romans 8:28 has been a special verse to me.

It became a "life verse" for me. It was as though God put that promise in the Bible just for me. Possibly it is connected to my early years and seeing God use the shame of sexual abuse to draw me to Himself.

Years later, after losing two sons and a grandson, Romans 8:28 is a hard verse to take in.

When confronted with this verse, I told God plainly that no good was good enough! As devastated parents, what are we to make of "all these things" that have happened in our lives? The traditional Christian viewpoint teaches that suffering has meaning. But what meaning can possibly come from our children's suffering and early death? What good can come to us as we suffer not only the pain of our children's suffering but our pain in losing them? The question of good coming from our sufferings is one of the most difficult questions for all people of faith. We all struggle at times with thinking, *How is God going to bring good out of this?* That's particularly true for those who have lost a child.

It is one thing to read about suffering, but it is quite another thing to experience it oneself. It is one thing to believe in God, and it is quite another thing to trust Him when looking at the still and lifeless bodies of our children. Perhaps the most difficult thing of all is to believe what the heart says above what the eye sees. God says to my heart, "Your son is alive! There is no death for believers!" My eye overrules my heart; my heart overrules my eye; my eye overrules my heart, and on and on like a young girl picking petals from a daisy. He loves me; he loves me not. And the beat goes on—full of faith one moment, full of doubt the next.

While not expecting the Christian life to be trouble-free, I didn't know to expect brokenness when Christ entered my heart with joy. When real suffering came, I experienced bitter disappointment in the Lord and also in myself. My loving and submissive attitude toward the Lord changed into a deep heart sickness and a demanding attitude.

"Where were You, God?" I demanded. "Did You plan this, or did You simply stand there and watch this tragedy unfold?"

I was disappointed in God for not doing my bidding. I had asked Him to take care of my children and protect them. He had failed me.

I have said earlier that I could not read grief books in the beginning. I had no interest in the suffering of others. It was only our loss that mattered. But I did read the Psalms. I read books on theology, trying to see where I had missed the God I thought I knew. I read the book of Job. And then, after reading the Lord's response to him, like Job, "I placed my hand on my mouth" (Job 40:4).

I was saddened, distressed, and disappointed in myself. I really thought I had loved God for His heart. I didn't know that I loved God for His hand, for what He could give to me and to those I loved. The Apostle Peter warns us, "Beloved, do not be surprised at the fiery ordeal among you, which comes upon you for your testing, as though some strange thing were happening to you" (1 Peter 4:12).

I knew that verse. I had studied it. I didn't think I could be fooled by the false doctrine that promises health and wealth in the name of Jesus. I thought I was above that kind of thinking. My Bible had taught me to expect suffering. But when death came for my children, it was too much. I was utterly shocked and undone. Had I been deceived? Maybe I had fallen for the misguided notion that a formula of faith exists: righteous living plus trust in God equals the good life now and heaven later.

Perhaps I thought I had the right to demand long lives for my children. With deep faith in a loving, sovereign heavenly Father, I assumed I had the right to believe He would safeguard my children from harm.

In *Notes to Myself*, Hugh Prather points out my error with these words during an illness his wife suffered:

> She may die before morning. But I have been with her for four years. There is no way I could feel cheated if I didn't have her for another day. I didn't deserve her for one minute, God knows. Few can choose when they will die. I choose to accept death now. As of this moment, I give up my "right" to live. And I give up my "right" to her life.
>
> But it's morning. I have been given another day. Another day to hear and read and smell and walk and love and glory. I am alive for another day. I think of those who aren't.[29]

When it comes to life and death, I never knew I had no rights. I had no rights to even be alive. I had no rights to the length of my children's lives, no rights to their presence, no rights to their future achievements, and no rights to my grandchildren who would never be born. God measures out the days, the hours, the minutes of our lives. Every year, every day, every hour, every moment of life is a gift.

The only appropriate response to a gift is gratitude. Choosing to be grateful doesn't take the pain away, but it does reframe our loss. Somehow it makes the suffering a little more bearable to remember our children are a gift. We can choose to be angry for the shortness of their lives or, while it is often difficult when grieving, we can be grateful that they had a chance at life. Alfred Lord Tennyson's words, "Though much is taken, much abides," are particularly relevant as we meditate on our good memories. Decades later, Garth Brooks echoed the sentiment in his song "The Dance," where he says, "I could have missed the pain, but I'd have had to miss the dance."

Eventually, we will agree with the poets and the artists that somehow, the pain has been a small price to pay for having had our beloved children, even for a short time. And our gratitude for those days, those treasured moments we shared, will increase with each passing year. Our memories are perhaps the most precious gifts we will ever possess.

After wrestling with the meaning of Romans 8:28 for many years—years of compounding loss upon loss—I am beginning to see the hope within this promise. God promises that He is at work in all our suffering world and bringing about a miraculous transformation.

Adrian Rogers, discussing Romans 8:28, says that salt is made of sodium and chloride. Each alone is a poison but mixed together; they create something altogether new. Combined, they create salt. We need that to live. That's how God works. He puts the bad things into the crucible of His love and makes them into something totally new and good. He makes something life-giving, even out of death. He is the living God who overcomes death. God is plotting a story of final good—a story of transformation for all of us.

C. S. Lewis writes that when we on earth say of some temporal suffering, "No future bliss can make up for it, not knowing that Heaven, once attained, will work backward and turn even that agony into a glory."[30]

I wish there were an easier way. I wish there was an obvious answer to all our questions. I wish children never died. But faced with reality, I must decide. Will I believe God's Word? And you must decide—will you believe God's Word? Does He love me, does He love you, or does He not?

Most of my friends and acquaintances who have lost children have drawn closer to their faith through the experience. Some have not. Some have chosen to deny the Lord's existence because they aren't able to believe in a good God any longer amid so much pain, suffering, and injustice. Some have settled for an independent path of the secular life, finding their fulfillment through earthly pleasures.

We must all decide for ourselves. I have decided. If God can bring Jesus back to life, if He can turn that terrible suffering of the cross to a good end, then I can trust Him to do something powerful and creative with my sufferings as well. I can trust Him with the lives and the deaths of my children. I have decided to live each day with an expectant heart, looking for the good that has come and will come from my losses.

Yes, I believe that God can and will create good out of even the worst evil. He has already done it once, so why not again? He says He will. I believe He will. I must rely upon Him and cling to His promises—day by day.

God says He is working for good to those who love Him and are called according to His purpose. He has not forgotten His original purpose. God is still working to create a people in His own image, just as He did from the beginning. In accepting His call that comes to all disciples to leave all and to come to Him, this promise of Romans 8:28 becomes personal to us. He not only is working on the external evil, but He is also changing us internally as well.

My journey of grief has been long and painful. I can say that I now see some good. Many people have come to the Lord because of our tragedies. Something has happened inside of us as well—Gary and I have changed. We enjoy the little things more. I love the sweetness of ordinary days, a sunrise, the first cup of coffee, the bloom of a flower.

I have accepted my limitations. I now know I can't fix things for those I love, but I can offer my shoulder, my listening ear, and my prayers.

The fact of the brevity and fragility of life is always before me. I overlook the faults in others more easily and pray more often. I am stronger in many ways but trust more in the Lord for my strength.

Gary and I don't hesitate to enter into the tragedies of others. We have learned to comfort with the comfort God gave us through others. We are more compassionate. Our faith is more rugged and enduring.

We have also learned the importance and discipline of waiting. This is essential for all of us, as we wait on God to work all things together for good. Waiting is always hard, but it has made us more patient. We aren't alone in our waiting. Abraham and Sarah had to wait on God and hope for a son when there was no reason left to hope. Joseph waited on God. He was sold as a slave, falsely accused, imprisoned, and forgotten before being raised up to second-in-command in Egypt, where he saved his family and many others. Moses waited on God, finally able to free his people as an old man. Hebrews 11 lists the names of suffering Saints who waited on God, trusting in His goodness even when God did not protect them from their trials. Like us, they were required to trust in the assurance of things unseen in their lifetimes.

Our Lord never gives us answers to our suffering, and we would probably not be satisfied by His answers if He did, for His ways are so beyond ours. The answers to our questions may come in time, or in time they may not even matter. Dostoevsky expressed this so well when he wrote:

> I believe like a child that suffering will be healed
> and made up for, that all the humiliating absurdity
> of human contradictions will vanish like a pitiful
> mirage—that in the world's finale, at the moment of
> eternal harmony, something so precious will come
> to pass that it will suffice for all hearts, for the com-
> forting of all resentments, for the atonement of all
> the crimes of humanity, of all the blood that they've
> shed; that it will make it not only possible to forgive
> but to justify all that happened.[31]

Like a child, I also believe.

Although you may not choose to listen to all the music recommended in each of these chapters, please take the time to listen to the selection for today. "Way Maker" is a song filled with reminders that we serve the living God, who is at work in our darkness to bring light. He is working, even when we don't see it. While still walking in darkness, while our sufferings and losses will continue to be a mystery, we must choose how to live today. Will we choose faith in God's character and His promises, or will we live by sight, trusting just what we see at the moment? Choose faith! There will come a day when the waiting will be over, when faith will become sight. Don't grow weary with waiting. Believe with me that God really is working "all things" together for good, for He is "able to do immeasurably more than all we ask or imagine" (Ephesians 3:20).

Prayer for Today

In brokenness, Lord, help me to surrender the illusion of my rights. Replace my demanding spirit with one of gratitude. You are the giver of all good gifts. Thank you. Thank you for my life. Thank you for my children's lives. Thank you for Your promise to bring good out of evil. I believe, Lord. Help me to rest on Your promises, waiting upon You to work it all out for good. I pray in the miracle-working name of Jesus, Amen.

CHAPTER TWENTY-TWO

Let's Dance: It's Time to Let Some Joy Back In

"You have turned my mourning into dancing for me; You have untied my sackcloth and encircled me with joy"

— Psalm 30:11

SONG TO HEAL YOUR HEART

"I Can Only Imagine"
by Mercy Me-One Voice Children's Choir

When Gary and I were dating, we often went out dancing. When our friends went to the movie and dinner, we were sipping cokes, kicking up our heels in country and western bars and small nightclubs.

My mother would have grounded me for life had she known, but we frequented a downtown bar on Forsythe Street in Beaumont called Shorty's Tavern. We were often the only white couple on the dance floor. Gary's neighbor was a police officer, and we only went when he was on duty for security. He would seat us up by the band in the light. We were quite popular with the clientele, and we loved their joyful dancing.

It was our privilege to listen and dance to Aretha Franklin, Little Anthony and the Imperials, and other great ascending artists.

As the music in our lives died with the deaths of our children, so did my ability to dance. If life is a dance, then the dance changed into a dirge for me. I moved slowly about the dance floor that was my life, dressed in black, weighed down as with leg irons. As time inched slowly onward and with the passage of many years, with my life's partner urging me forward, I found the courage to step back onto the dance floor.

My husband often reminds me, "We've got to keep dancing."

And it's true. There does come a time to begin to live again.

There comes a day when your first thought upon awakening will not be of your loss. There comes a day when the future holds a brightness that is difficult to deny. But it is our choice. Acceptance is the magic that frees us. With acceptance comes the courage to move forward and to live despite the pain and loss. As Vivian Greene said, "Life isn't about waiting for the storm to pass. It's about learning to dance in the rain."

We must find new purposes and allow pleasure to return. It is an important time in our grief work. To release our hold on our children feels like a betrayal. But it is not. It is the progression God intends for us. For there is "A time to weep and a time to laugh; a time to mourn and a time to dance" (Ecclesiastes 3:4).

We must go forward, fixing our thoughts on "Whatever is true, whatever is honorable, whatever is right, whatever is pure, whatever is lovely, whatever is commendable, if there is any excellence and if anything worthy of praise, think about these things… and the God of peace will be with you" (Philippians 4:8–9).

While we will never get answers to our tragedy and suffering, by the grace of God, we can find meaning. While we will never understand the why of our journey, we cannot question the fact of the transformation that has taken place inside of us.

Jim Branch, in his book *Watch and Wait*, puts it this way:

> Who would've imagined that the groans and cries
> and tears and struggle would have brought us to
> that place; that place where our hearts were both
> broken and expanded, where our souls were both
> crushed and deepened beyond measure. Who
> could've dreamt that the effects of the fire and the
> water would have been to make us more like Jesus—
> *who suffers with* and delivers, he who *weeps over* and
> heals?[32]

Nothing that happens is wasted, but all will be woven into God's plan for changing us into His likeness.

My husband and I have taken tens of thousands of portraits of people. My husband photographed four US presidents, six vice presidents, the prime minister of England, generals, governors, sports figures, movie stars, and our favorite, families. Our life's work is archived at Lamar University in Beaumont, Texas, as The Life and Times of the People of Southeast Texas.

When a person would come in to sit for a portrait, there were usually two kinds of clients. One kind would arrive with photographs from an earlier time, showing the best angle of their face and the desired expression. During the sitting, they would resist direction, refuse to turn away from their imagined best side, often resulting in an awkward and stiff appearance.

And then there was the second kind of client, who would arrive with no plan laid out for us to follow. They would just relax in our hands, trusting that since we were the ones who could see most clearly, they could trust us to achieve the best for them. And Gary might say, "Tilt your head a little," for he knows the most flattering angle for any face is with the face slightly turned toward one side (since looking directly at the camera can tend to flatten the face). And the person would obey. And he might say, "Now lean forward on your right arm, and lift your face a bit" (knowing but not saying that a forward lean with a lifted chin could reduce the appearance of a double chin). And forward, they would lean.

I imagine we approach God in a similar way. Many of us are determined to become the person we want to be and intend to be. We disregard His plan. We ignore His leading and admonitions. We resist the Spirit and combat His plan, certain that we know what is best.

Perhaps if we were wise, we would just rest in His hands, following His leading and listening to His Word. Like the wise photographic client, we would realize that He can see more clearly than we. We would understand He has a purpose for us and has set about making it happen.

Do we glorify God by accepting that all we go through, all our suffering, is being used to make us more like Christ? We can believe the words of the Apostle Paul, "We are afflicted in every way, but not crushed; perplexed, but not despairing, persecuted but not abandoned; struck down, but not destroyed; always carrying around in the body the dying of Jesus, so that the life of Jesus may also be revealed in our mortal flesh" (2 Corinthians 4:8–12).

God has placed a worthy goal in front of all of us. We are called to be like Him.

Dr. Robert Rainy was a Scottish Presbyterian divine in the late 1800s. His words of generations ago say it so well. "Do you believe your faith? Do you believe what I am telling you? Do you believe a day is coming, really coming, when you will stand before the throne of God, and the angels will whisper together and say, 'Oh, how like Christ he is'?"

Now that will be a reason to dance!

Prayer for Today

Father, fill us with the joy of our salvation. Give us the strength to surrender our sorrow, to rise from grief, and to live our lives to the full, joyfully, even as we watch the clouds awaiting Your return. Maranatha. Come quickly, Lord Jesus. Amen.

CHAPTER TWENTY-THREE

Lift up Your Eyes: Draw Courage from Knowing Your Story Has Just Begun

"He will wipe away every tear from their eyes; and there will no longer be any death; there will no longer be any mourning, or crying, or pain; the first things have passed away.

And He who sits on the throne said, 'Behold, I am making all things new!' And he said, 'Write, for these words are faithful and true.'"

— Revelations 21:4–5

SONG TO HEAL YOUR HEART

"My Story" (Official Music Video) by Big Daddy Weave

My husband endured a kidney stone recently. If you've ever suffered from one yourself or heard someone tell of the ordeal, you know how excruciating a kidney stone can be.

Arriving at the emergency room, Gary was asked about his pain level.

"On a scale of one to ten," the nurse inquired, "tell me how much pain you're in."

"Nine," he replied through gritted teeth as our eyes met.

"You look like a ten to me, sir," the nurse responded.

His face etched with pain, he shook his head and repeated, "Nine."

We know what level-ten pain feels like. And so do you.

I don't know where you are on your grief journey, but I hope your pain level is decreasing. It is a sliding scale with many ups and downs. Time will be your ally. At some point, we must learn to face our world as it is—not as we wish it to be. As for me, I am a slow griever. It has taken more years than I can count to come to peace with our losses.

We have all learned that life is not permanent. We do, however, have hope. There is a time coming when "every tear will be wiped from our eyes." A new world is coming. There will be reunion and, as Timothy Keller says, "Love without parting." Christ does not ask us to deceive ourselves and to stop feeling or looking at the reality of our lives. What Christ promises is a living power to be present with us. We are to be honest in our pain, knowing that God is patient, kind, and understanding.

In spite of our losses and our sorrows, to a great degree, all of us are responsible for who we become. How we feel is not who we are. What matters is not so much what becomes of us but who we become.

In the Book of Ruth, Naomi returns to Jerusalem after losing her two sons and her husband. Her very name means "pleasant." Upon her arrival back home, Naomi changes her name to Mara, meaning "bitter." We can make that choice too, for it is ours to make. We are free to decide how to respond to our suffering. Will we change our name to "Bitter," or we will we choose to be renamed "Oaks of Righteousness," planted by God to display His glory? (Isaiah 61:3, NRSV).

As I see it, there are two kinds of suffering—suffering with no purpose and suffering with purpose. Our suffering can have a purpose, for our stories of loss and sadness can, in the end, tell a tale of the redeemer who is faithful and true. We have much to decide, you and me, about how it will all end.

I have often watched vivacious and smiling women from afar with a bit of envy, wondering what their lives were like. What would I be like if I had not seen so much sorrow? Would I be more fun, more interesting, more attractive? Would I have accomplished more? I have grieved over what appear to be the "lost years" of my life, years spent in sorrow, mourning, and depression. You know those days and years as well—tear-stained years of heartbreak and disappointment, years yearning for your child.

Hearing me express these regrets over my lost years, a close friend asked, "Could you have done anything differently?"

And, of course, the answer was "no." I did the best I could at the time, under the circumstances.

It doesn't sound like a story of victory, does it?

For many years, I felt deeply confused about the Lord's dealing. If you remember, at the beginning of this book, I asked the Lord to choose His best for me. And then my life imploded. The Lord answered my questions through Buel Kazee, who wrote these words for me that God had spoken to him: "Faith is not trusting me to get something; faith is trusting me when there seems to be nothing left. When everything is gone with no hope of restoration and when there is nothing on which to base your faith, then can you still trust Me?"[33]

I thought faith would bring victory, but I was mistaken. I came to see, through my tears, that *"faith is* the victory." Taking stock of my faith, I could see that I still believed. As the Apostle John said, "This is the victory that has overcome the world: our faith" (1 John 5:4).

Although I still look and watch for God to work a miracle for us, perhaps the greatest miracle has already been worked in us. We believe in spite of everything.

Then I read this promise: "And the Lord said to me, 'I will restore to you the years which the locust hath eaten'" (Joel 2:25, KJV).

God can give back all those years of sorrow, and we will be the better for them. Will a day come when we shall have to thank God for all this sadness of heart? It is a strange story and hard to believe, but it is the promise of God. He says He will bring good for us out of our black nights. Jesus was anointed to proclaim the good news of God's grace. He was sent to bind up our broken hearts, to free the captives and release from the darkness all the prisoners, to comfort all who mourn. Yes, the Lord sets the captives free, even those of us in prisons of our own making. We are dear children of God who have been one, ten, or twenty years the bearers of despair. This promise will, in the fullness of time, be sweetly fulfilled for us and our children:"I will restore unto you the years which the locust have eaten."

The idea of each of our lives being a "story" is not a new one. In his memoir *Telling Secrets*, Frederick Buechner states:

My story is important not because it is mine, God knows, but because if I tell it anything like right, the chances are you will recognize that in many ways, it is also yours… It is precisely through these stories in all their particularity, as I have long believed and often said, that God makes himself known to each of us more powerfully and personally. If this is true, it means that to lose track of our stories is to be profoundly impoverished, not only humanly but also spiritually.[34]

I have been thinking of you and praying for you as you have read my story. It is my earnest prayer that God will use these words to make Himself known to you more powerfully and personally, that He will touch your broken heart and reveal His great love for you and your child. The living God, our Father, has a plan for the ages that includes you and me, your loves and mine.

In closing, I want to share with you this quote by C. S. Lewis. It is the words of the Christ figure, Aslan the lion, as he paints a portrait of the future, pointing to the end of our unfinished stories.

And as He spoke, He no longer looked to them like a lion; but the things that began to happen after that were so great and beautiful that I cannot write them. And for us, this is the end of all the stories, and we can most truly say that they all lived happily ever after. But for them, it was only the beginning

of the real story. All their life in this world and all
their adventures in Narnia had only been the cover
and the title page: now, at last, they were beginning
Chapter One of the Great Story which no-one on
earth has read; which goes on forever; in which
every chapter is better than the one before.[35]

We have lived only the cover and the title page of our stories.
While tragedy is a part of the stories of our lives, it need not
define us. The resurrection of Christ changes everything. It
provides all the hope we need in life and in death. We will soon
enter into Chapter One of the Great Story of love and reunion
when all things will be made new, when all things cut short on
earth will be completed and restored to us and to our children.
Trust Him. He will redeem the past, the present, and the future.

Let us press on to know the Lord whose name is Faithful and
True, for His soon return is as certain as the dawn.

Prayer for Today

God of miracles, tune our aching hearts to the music of Your
love. Give us light for our darkness, peace for our fear, joy for
our sorrow. Renew Your spirit within our hearts and give us the
grace to wait upon You to write Your story of redemption and
restoration with our lives. Amen.

The Early Years: Childhood Hardships Build Resilience for Later Heartaches

Thank you for picking up this book and taking the time to read it. It is my great hope that you have found thoughts within these pages to soothe your pain.

As a fellow griever, I still stumble and blunder through life. I have not arrived, but I have survived. Perhaps I am more experienced at navigating the path of grief because of repetition and time. I have learned that although we walk a lonely path, we do not have to walk it alone.

To finish our time together, I want to share with you my early years, when I first experienced the reality of the living God and began to walk with Him.

* * *

The philosopher Soren Kierkegaard said, "Life can only be understood backwards, but it must be lived forwards." As I look back and ponder my early life, God's invisible hand becomes visible. I now see the painful and difficult events of those early years prepared me to survive the grief that lay ahead. It was in those years as the Lord revealed His love for me that I learned to hear His voice in my spirit and to recognize His presence. It was in those years of desperate prayers and long-awaited answers that I learned to trust the Lord.

Simply put, my early years of heartache and confusion—along with a newfound faith in God—prepared me for the deep sorrow that would come years later.

As a child, I knew what we all know as children—that we were created to live happily ever after. But something must have gone wrong. In disappointment, I asked myself, "Is this really my life, or has there been some mistake?"

My mother and my dad had married during World War II. Mother was a math and science teacher and older than Daddy. It has always been a mystery how they ever got together, but somehow, they did.

Daddy never finished high school, instead enlisting in the military. After six years in the military, fighting in North Africa and at Normandy, he left the service as a master sergeant. My brother was born during the war years.

After my father returned home, he moved in with Mother's parents, where she and my brother were living. My grandfather, who we knew as Papaw, owned a 250-acre farm about seven miles outside of Tylertown, Mississippi. He raised cattle, ran a dairy, and grew enough food to feed a small village. The plan was for Daddy to help Papaw run the farm. But my dad had a much different vision for the farm. After a disagreement over some improvement, my daddy went to town and didn't return. Mother soon discovered that Daddy had taken all their money out of the bank before disappearing.

I was born several months later. My mother was staying with her sister in Hattiesburg, Mississippi, where I was born. Mother was in a desperate situation.

When I was six weeks old, my dad contacted my mother and, against the advice of her parents, she made the long trip from Mississippi to Houston, Texas, with my two-year-old brother and me in tow. They wanted to try again to make their marriage work. Daddy had bought a house and had a job driving a potato chip truck. After several years, he found an opportunity with the Borden's Milk Company, and we all moved to Beaumont, Texas. Things went well for a while. With Mother managing the money, they began buying milk trucks and built the business up to five routes, with additional drivers hired to help.

When I was eight years old, one of my daddy's relatives moved in with us for a while to work for him. My parents never knew it, but when this man moved in, the dark reality of sexual abuse moved into my life. I was filled with shame. My home was not a safe place.

In my middle school days, my dad drank too much and yelled a lot. Mother fretted and worried. I remember dozing under my blanket in the back seat of our car as Mother drove us around late at night to beer joints. She would send my brother in to look for Daddy.

We were all afraid of Daddy's anger. He was a terrible hot head. My heart filled with guilt because of my brother, who bore the brunt of the punishment. If he did something wrong, Daddy whipped him. If I did something wrong, Daddy whipped him for not stopping me. Every night, I prayed that Daddy would quit drinking and smoking. I prayed that my parents would love one another.

We didn't have any family close by, and my parents did not socialize with any friends, so we grew up rather isolated. I never asked friends over to the house because I never knew what to expect.

When we were old enough, Mother took my brother and me to the local Baptist church, dropping us off for Sunday school.

One day, when I was twelve, I sat in the tent at South Park Baptist Church in Beaumont. The church house had recently burned down, so the tent served as the place of worship. I listened to a visiting missionary talk about the conditions in South America, describing the conditions in Chile by using the word chaos over and over. I had heard the word before but did not really understand its meaning. As he continued to explain the conditions in that country, I began to understand that he was also describing the conditions in my own home, my own family, my own heart. And then he went on to prescribe a cure: Trust in the one who could calm the chaos and the fear. He talked about an all-knowing Father—who knew all about me and loved me anyway.

He spoke of a Father who is strong and eager to save those who trusted in Him.

The speaker told about the Father's only son, Jesus, who could take all my sins—and even the sins of others against me—upon Himself as the punishment for all. He paid my debt, and He died in my place so that I could live and be free. He said that Jesus came for the weak and not for the strong. He came for those who were ashamed and not for the proud.

And then the missionary said that anyone who wanted to receive a new life could come forward to the front. I went forward. I thought no one could want a new life more than me.

And you know what happened? I received that new life he spoke about.

It was my first taste of joy. My new hero, Jesus, took away all my shame and guilt. He took away all my grief and baptized me with gladness.

Though my heart and inner life had changed dramatically, my home life had not changed much. In a lot of ways, things got worse. Even as family life continued to be chaotic, I had peace on the inside. Never again in those days was I hopeless or alone. Constantly, I prayed that my parents would love one another. But the turmoil persisted. Daddy had come and gone so often in those years that we never knew what to expect from him. I usually wished he was home when he was gone and wished he was gone when he was home.

When I was a junior in high school, our house caught fire. The top story of the house burned, and the downstairs was flooded. We were moved into an apartment provided by the insurance company. Daddy dropped us at the apartment, drove to our burned-out house, and took everything of value he could find. He then disappeared once again, returning four months later after the house was rebuilt.

Finally, when I was a senior in high school, my parents divorced. It was the great "ahhhh" of my life. There was peace. I still loved my daddy but not the man he had become.

As time went on and with my dad remarried, we saw less and less of him. Daddy had long stopped contributing to the family finances. With Mother's modest teaching salary, she saved and scrimped like many single mothers, somehow sending my brother and me through college.

Years later—when I was married with four children—my mother contracted breast cancer. I was her primary caregiver for more than nine years. After her first surgery and treatment, she went into remission for a while. When the cancer returned, we sold her house and leased the one behind us, so I could watch over her more closely. At the same time, unknown to us, Daddy was diagnosed with cancer of the larynx.

Mother, Daddy, and I were shocked at their first radiation treatment to find ourselves all together in the waiting room at the Mamie McFaddin Ward Cancer Treatment Center. God had arranged for their treatments to be only minutes apart in the local cancer center. For weeks, my mother and daddy met and talked in the waiting room while they took turns having their treatments. My dad got better; my mother got worse.

Daddy started to call her every day on the phone. Sometimes he would drop by her house to drink coffee and to talk. When she could no longer drive, Mother gave her car to him. When we got to the point that she could not be left alone, I would call Daddy to come sit with her when I needed a break. I was amazed to see God answering my childhood prayers—decades later—as they hugged and patted one another.

At her funeral, my dad stood beside me with tears running down his face. "I loved her," he said. "You know that."

"Yes, Daddy," I said, hugging him. "I know."

Daddy's cancer recurred in his lungs a year later. I sat with him during his last bedridden days. I was never proud of how he lived, but I was awfully proud of how he faced his death. It was good to see the man he had become—full of faith, courage, humor, and love for those around him.

Sometimes it is good to look back and remember our own stories and to look for the presence of God between the pages. I now think my first dramatic knowledge of God's love for me and His faithfulness in answering prayers for my parents proved important for all that was to come my way.

Pain and hardship in our past are a preparation for today. No, I'm not saying I was prepared to lose a child. There is nothing that prepares a parent for such a loss. It is beyond the imagination. What I am saying is that resilience is achieved through all our sufferings. God knows the path our lives will take even before we are born. Our early years are never wasted. You are stronger than you know. Past experiences lay a foundation that gives hope and assurance that survival is possible even in the worst of times.

Although for many years God's work was hidden and silent in my life, I knew that He was near. Knowing that the Lord is near and that heaven's work is a reality in our daily lives can't help but bring a calm confidence to us as believers in the Most High God.

What about you? When looking back over your life, can you see the presence of Jesus? Do you remember when God wooed you to Himself? Do you remember the experience of answered prayers and words of guidance in confusing times? The same God who heard and answered the prayers of His people long ago continues to hear our prayers today. God doesn't change.

As you ponder your own journey to where you find yourself today, be reassured by the words of author Ken Gire: "God's love for us, not ours for him, is the rope around our waist. It is a rope that does not fray, no matter how it is stretched. It does not freeze, no matter how cold it gets. It does not fail, no matter how far we fall—or how often."[36]

ABOUT THE AUTHOR

Moving to Texas from Mississippi at six weeks of age, Cheryl considers herself a Texan. A graduate of Lamar University in Beaumont, Texas, she has spent her life being a wife, a mother of four, and grandmother to eight. Although most of her professional career involves working as a photo stylist and creating exceptional portraiture, events, and personalized artwork, her life has had many facets.

Cheryl modeled professionally for the Ben Shaw Agency in Houston, Texas. As a marketing executive, she created fashion programs marketing to women in the legal field both in Beaumont and Houston. Creating a business presenting others at their best, she presented wardrobe shows, assisted women in wardrobe selections and etiquette classes.

Cheryl launched a successful bridal line, Christopher & LaLou, soliciting investors, constructing a collaboration with foreign designers, co-designing, and marketing internationally. She secured editorials in *Bride's*, *Manhattan Bride*, *Bridal Guide*, as well as European and Japanese fashion magazines. A gown by Christopher & LaLou graced the cover of *Modern Bride* and was selected as the logo gown for the first March on Madison for brides by the Conde' Nast Magazine Group. Cheryl forged a collaboration with LaLique in Paris, creating and marketing the only bridal collection embellished with LaLique crystals. These gowns were carried exclusively by Saks Fifth Avenue.

As a follower of Christ since childhood, Cheryl, along with her husband, has always been involved in community and ministry. She has taught, organized, and launched numerous impactful ministries for youth and for women.

Through the years, Cheryl's talents have given her the opportunity to speak to groups— large and small—for spiritual inspiration.

Cheryl's days are spent celebrating life through writing, painting, speaking, and entertaining in Bryan, Texas, where she shares life with her husband, Gary Christopher, two children, and seven grandchildren, all residing within the great state of Texas.

The author can be reached at cherylchristopherauthor.com.

ENDNOTES

[1] "Words for It" from *The Artist's Way: A Spiritual Path to Higher Creativity* by Julia Cameron, copyright 1992, 2002 by Julia Cameron. Used by permission of Tarcher, an imprint of Penguin Publishing Group, a division of Penguin Random House LLC. All rights reserved.

[2] Hannah Hurnard, *Hinds' Feet on High Places* (Carol Stream, Ill.: Tyndale House, 1975), 52.

[3] Buell H. Kazee, *Faith is The Victory* (Wheaton, Ill.: Tyndale House, 1983), 141.

[4] Paul David Tripp, *Suffering* (Wheaton, Ill.: Crossway, 2018), 23.

[5] Larry Crabb, *Inside Out* (Colorado Springs, Colo.: Navpress, 1988), 77.

[6] Claudia Gray, *A Thousand Pieces of You* (New York: HarperCollins, 2014), 143.

[7] Joseph Bayly, *The View from a Hearse* (Bloomington, IN.: Clearmont Press, 2014), 41.

[8] Danielle Bernock, *Emerging With Wings* (4F Media, 2014), 154.

[9] C. S. Lewis, *A Grief Observed* (New York: Harper Collins Publishers, 1994), 3.

[10] Paul David Tripp, *Suffering: Gospel Hope When Life Doesn't Make Sense* (Wheaton Ill.: Crossway, 2018), 62.

[11] Ann and Jeanette Petrie, producers and directors, *Mother Teresa* (Petrie Productions, 1986).

[12] Jerry White, *I Will Not Be Broken* (New York: St. Martin's Press, 2008),117.

[13] Unison Prayer Center for Christian Ethics Baylor University

[14] Henri Nouwen, *Gracias* (New York, N.Y. Harper & Row, 1983), 82.

[15] Ken Gire, *The North Face of God* (Wheaton, Ill.: Tyndale House, 2005), 40.

[16] Nick Trout, *Tell Me Where It Hurts* (New York: Broadway Books, 2008), 10.

[17] Frederick Buechner, *Telling Secrets* (San Francisco:Harper San Francisco, 1991), 49.

[18] Jim Branch, " Pieces," *The Blue Book* (Lexington, KY: CreateSpace, 2017). 372–373. Used by permission of the author.

[19] Lloyd J. Ogilvie, *Asking God Your Hardest Questions* (Colorado Springs, CO: WaterBrook Press, 1996), 42.

[20] Ibid.

[21] J. B. Phillips, *Your God Is Too Small* (New York, N.Y., the MacMillan Company,1961), 118–119.

[22] Jim Branch, *The Blue Book* (Lexington, KY,CreateSpace, 2017), 17.

23 John Green, *The Fault In Our Stars* (New York, N.Y., The Penguin Group, 2012), 262.

24 Carla Fine, *No Time to Say Goodbye*, (New York: Doubleday, 1997), 36 citing The Diagnostic and Statistical Manual of Mental Disorders, 4th ed. (DSM-IV) (Washington, D.C.: American Psychiatric Association, 1994).

25 C. S. Lewis, *A Grief Observed* (New York, N.Y. HarperCollins,1961), 5–6.

26 Jonathan Evans, 1/8/2020, Jonathan Evans Delivers Viral Eulogy of His Mother Lois, retrieved from https://lifewayresearch.com.

27 Fredrick Buechner, *The Sacred Journey* (New York:Harper & Row, 1982), 100.

28 Lloyd J. Ogilvie, *Asking God Your Hardest Questions* (Colorado Springs, CO, 1981), 83.

29 Hugh Prather, *Notes to Myself* (New York: Bantam Books, 1990).

30 C. S. Lewis, *The Great Divorce, A Dream* (London: Geoffrey Bles, 1946), 69.

31 Fyodor Dostoyevsky, *The Brothers Karamazov* (New York: Vintage Books, 1950), 308.

32 Jim Branch, *Watch and Wait* (New York: Create Space Independent Publishing, 2015), 56.

33 Buel H.Kazee, *Faith Is The Victory* (Wheaton, Ill.: Tyndale House,1983), 149.

[34] Frederick Buechner, *Telling Secrets* (New York: HarperCollins,1991), 30.

[35] C. S. Lewis, *The Last Battle, The Chronicles of Narnia* (New York: Harper Trophy, 1956), 228.

[36] Ken Gire, *The North Face of God* (Wheaton, Ill.: Tyndale House), 16.